HOPE ISLAND

HOPE ISLAND

LORI BOYD

START2FINISH

ISBN-10: 1944704450
ISBN-13: 978-1944704452

Published by Start2Finish
Fort Worth, Texas 76244
www.start2finish.org

Printed in the United States of America

Cover Design: Josh Feit, Evangela.com

TO SAM, EVIE,
KATE, AND BRIGGS

I love being with you,
learning with you,
laughing with you,
and hoping with you.

ACKNOWLEDGMENTS

AS WITH EVERY WRITING PROJECT, there are many hands that touched and shaped the process from beginning to end. I'd like to take a moment to recognize a few special people who helped me develop this study.

The idea for *Hope Island* took root at a ladies' retreat I attended in East Tennessee, hosted by the Chickamauga church of Christ. Our subject for the weekend was "Anchored by Hope." For one small group activity, the ladies—pretending to be shipwreck survivors—took poster boards and created communities based on HOPE: the confident expectation that they would be rescued. When the poster boards were lined up on the wall at the front of the room, something extraordinary was revealed. I remember talking through each island community and then turning to the group and saying, "This!…(motioning to the line of posters)…This is what the church should look like!"

On my drive home, as I reflected on that activity, I knew I had to write about it. So, thank you to my sisters who attended that retreat, for your kindness and for your inspiration. I arrived that weekend not knowing a single soul and left two days later with hugs and tears and feeling like I was leaving family—just the way it should be in the church.

I thank my precious family: my husband, Sam, and my children, Evie, Kate, and Briggs. They are patient, gracious, and kind. I couldn't be a writer without having their help and encouragement. They give me endless ideas and infinite inspiration. I love them with my whole heart.

I also thank my publisher, Michael Whitworth, and my editor, Kristy Hinson. I love them both for their support, their guidance, and their wisdom. But all of that aside, I love them even more for their examples of faith and for being my friends.

Above all, I thank God for his grace, mercy, and love. I thank him for establishing his kingdom, for giving us his Word, and for the hope of his Son's return. I humbly pray that he guide my steps according to his Will, and that I live my life to his honor and glory.

TABLE OF CONTENTS

Where it Begins
THE TALE OF A FATEFUL TRIP 11

Chapter 1
FIRST, WE FIND WATER! 20
Set priorities

Chapter 2
DISCOVER AND EXPLORE! 34
Grow in knowledge

Chapter 3
ALL FOR ONE AND ONE FOR ALL! 46
Be unified

Chapter 4
BUILDERS, AND FISHERS, AND COOKS...OH MY! 58
Recognize talents and abilities

Chapter 5
WE'RE NOT THE ONLY ONES HERE! 71
Share the message

Chapter 6
WE HAVE A MAN DOWN! 84
Help each other

Chapter 7
PUT OUT THAT FIRE! 97
Seek peace

Chapter 8

YOU CAN DO THIS!... 111

Be encouraging

Chapter 9

LIVING HERE IS HARD! 124

Expect persecution

Chapter 10

QUITTING IS NOT AN OPTION! 140

Don't give up

Chapter 11

A HALF-FULL COCONUT! 154

Find joy

Chapter 12

THERE'S TREASURE HERE! 168

Discover extraordinary love

Chapter 13

DON'T GET ATTACHED TO THE ISLAND!........................ 180

Remember your home

Epilogue 193

THE TALE OF
A FATEFUL TRIP

THE STORM

There had been no sign of rain. The sky had been completely unfurnished. It had been "smooth sailing," if you will. Until now.

The hull of the boat crashed through angry waves and water began to fill the upper and lower decks. Darkness had torn through the heavenly veil and brought with it black clouds bursting with rain. Lightning ripped across the sky. Thunder shook the ocean. The wind raged and billows rose higher and higher.

The black radio in the captain's cabin had been the ship's connection to the shore. Since the sudden turn of the weather, several desperate messages had been sent notifying the coast guard of their situation. So far there had been no response. Did the messages even go through? Was anyone aware of what was happening to the crew of the *S.S. Sarx*? It appeared that they were on their own. Sink or swim? Live or die? Which would it be?

The forty passengers, who thirty minutes ago had been enjoying a beautiful day at sea, were now fighting to survive a storm. It had been two days since their feet had last touched solid ground, and two days since their eyes had last seen it. The fear that filled every head was the possibility that they would never touch land or see it again. The boat was breaking apart right beneath them. Staying on course was hopeless, but nobody cared. Staying alive was now the mission.

Lifeboats were dropped, and life vests were secured. Desperate hands grabbed survival supplies. Piece by piece the boat began to sink below the surface and one by one, men, women, and children were pulled from the water onto the inflatable rafts.

Side by side the passengers sat, faces down, backs bent over, and arms intertwined. The storm muted the coughing, sobbing, and loud prayers pleading for mercy. Only the captain sat still and tall. Only he knew something the rest of the crew did not. Only he had heard the three broken, static-woven words that tripped through the radio just as water flooded his cabin: **"Rescue is coming."**

He would tell the others as soon as they were safe. And he believed with all of his heart that they would be.

THE SURVIVORS

"Everyone come! Come over here!" the captain called out.

As he looked across the shore, he could see all four lifeboats and he quickly began to register each survivor. Some people were still in the boats, some were lying in the sand, and others were wandering aimlessly around the beach.

"Let me get a headcount!" he yelled.

Slowly, they began to circle around him.

"One…two…three…four…" he counted

"…twenty-five…twenty-six…twenty-seven…"

"…thiry-eight…thirty-nine…and I make forty."

Forty survivors. Three days drifting since the storm and *every single passenger had survived.*

The captain asked each person to take the hands of those standing next to them and he led them all in a prayer of praise and thanksgiving. Many dropped to their knees and lowered their heads to the sand. Tears fell down each face. At the close of the prayer, one small voice, weighted with fear and with exhaustion, asked the question that filled every heart… "What do we do now?"

"We live," the captain answered, "until we are rescued."

"But how do you know we will be rescued?" someone called out from the circle.

"There was a message," he explained. "It came through on the radio just before the ship went down. The message was that 'rescue is coming.' They know what happened to us and they will come for us. In the meantime, we will continue to survive. We will live here, knowing that it won't be home for very long. We will build a community together and it will thrive on hope."

With those words, the survivors got to work.

THE ISLAND

If you looked back at the island from the edge of the water, it looked empty. Yes, there were trees, hills, rocks, and sand; but there was no sign of human life. The forty survivors seemed to be alone. How would they survive?

"Rescue is coming."

That promise would sustain them. It would become their mantra.
They would sink into those words and rise out of despair again and again.

No matter what challenges they would face on the island, they would remember "rescue is coming" and that message would give them hope.

The survivors looked forward to the day a ship would come to take them home, and that hope defined their everyday life on the island. They began to create a community based on their impending rescue. The result was Hope Island: a destination as reachable as it was remote; as life-changing as it was challenging; and as precious as it was peculiar.

This is where our study begins.

A DIFFERENT KIND OF HOPE

HOPE IN THE WORLD

What is hope? When we hear the word "hope" used in the world today, it often carries with it the idea of "wishful thinking" or the belief that something "may or may not" happen. We might say something like, "I sure hope the weather will be nice while we're on vacation" or "I hope this new job opportunity comes through." We use the word "hope" with a sort of watered down anticipation, like a dream whispered with fingers crossed and eyes closed. "I hope…" could refer to something we want, or even expect, but not with the *certainty* that our desire will be fulfilled. Hope in the world is fleeting—here one day and gone the next. It's ever-changing and varies in degree of gravity— from the trivial (I hope someone brought a chocolate pie to the potluck) to the crucial (I hope I'm able to endure this new diagnosis). This hope can be frustrating, disappointing, and even heart-breaking.

This is not the same hope that cost the apostle Paul his freedom (Acts 28:20).

This is not the same hope that is present in death (Prov. 14:32).

And it is not the same hope that is found in God (Psa. 71:5).

Hope that is found in the world is not the same hope we read about on the pages of our Bibles.

AN INFINITELY BETTER HOPE

The hope that we read about in the New Testament is defined as a "confident expectation" and a "happy anticipation." It carries with it the idea of trust. It's not weak-kneed or wavering, but constant and assured. As Christians, what is it that we are confidently expecting? What are we happily anticipating? The answer can be found in Titus 2:11-14:

"For the grace of God that brings salvation has appeared to all men, teaching us that, denying ungodliness and worldly lusts, we should live soberly, righteously, and godly in the present age, looking for the blessed hope and glorious appearing of our great God and Savior Jesus Christ, who gave Himself for us, that He might redeem us from every lawless deed and purify for Himself His own special people, zealous for good works."

In that text, the word "hope" is translated from the Greek word *elpis*, meaning "expectation of what is sure, or certain." For the faithful follower of Christ, hope is the joyful and confident expectation of eternal salvation. It's the anticipation of Jesus coming back one day to take his family home. It's complete trust in Jesus' redeeming power and God's gracious gift of salvation. It's a hope that is worth living for and worth dying for. It's a fixture in the life of Christians that sets them apart from the world.

THE SURVIVORS AND THE CHURCH

The survivors on Hope Island share a common hope: the hope of rescue.

They know that rescue is coming; they just don't know when. But until it does, their hope will keep them alive. In fact, it won't just keep them alive; it will allow them to thrive as a community of people working together for a collective purpose. Their hope is reflected in the way they daily live on the island, from the physical work they do to the relationships they have with each other. The hope they have for the future influences their thoughts, their actions, and even their character.

There are many lessons to be learned from Hope Island, especially if we consider the survivors to be a representation of the church. First, it's important to understand that the Bible teaches there are two aspects of salvation in this life: present salvation from our sins (Eph. 1:13; 2:5) and then a future salvation that will be revealed when Jesus comes again (1 Pet. 1:5; Acts 15:11). As a group of people who have been saved by the grace of God through his Son, Jesus Christ, and who have accepted his gift of salvation through our faithful obedience, we now have hope for eternal life. We have a hope that we, like the Hope Island survivors, will be rescued. One day we will look up and see Jesus in the sky. We know he's coming, we just don't know when; but until he does, our hope sustains us and strengthens us.

This study explores characteristics of life on Hope Island and discusses how those characteristics should be reflected in the church. Each chapter begins with a look at the attitudes or behaviors of the island survivors under the heading, "The Survivors," and is followed by a section entitled "The Church," which applies those same attitudes and behaviors to Christians in the world today from a biblical perspective. The chapters are titled by island principles as well as corresponding spiritual principles.

THE JOURNAL

In the course of their first day on Hope Island, the survivors discover a collection of writings from a former shipwreck survivor who had kept a journal of his experiences on the island. The writings come in the form of a daily log and the information they find there proves to be invaluable to their continued survival. You'll recognize the wisdom communicated in those logs as it comes from none other than the most famous shipwreck survivor in Scripture: the apostle Paul!

Paul's New Testament letters are sprinkled with affirmations of hope, messages regarding the Truth, and instructions on how to live as followers of Christ. The author of the journal found on Hope Island, a man also by the name of Paul, wrote concerning the comforts and the dangers he experienced while there. His advice and his cautions are taken to heart by the recent survivors and they benefit greatly from his wisdom. At the end of "The Journal" section, there are Scripture references from the apostle Paul's letters that correlate with the thoughts expressed in the daily log.

Once the journal has been found, it becomes a part of the survivors' daily lives and is read every morning when the group comes together. Starting and continuing from chapter two, the journal entry is the first section of each chapter because the words written there guide the survivors from day to day.

THE SPYGLASS

Imagine the world has a spyglass and people are looking at the church through the lens. What do they see? Do they see a community filled with hope? Do they see people who are confident in their salvation? Are our actions consistent with our belief that we are going to heaven? What should the world see when it looks at the church?

If we, as Christians, whole-heartedly anticipate the return of Jesus, and if we truly expect salvation, then when the world sees us, they should see the most joyful, loving, and freely forgiving people. They should see kind-hearted people who work together, who encourage each other, and who can't wait to share the good news about Jesus.

In this portion of each lesson, we'll consider what the world sees when it comes to the spiritual principle being discussed in that chapter. What is the world's view of the church through the spyglass and is that consistent with what the Bible tells us it should be?

THE REFLECTIONS

In this section of each chapter there is a list of questions related to the subject being addressed. These questions can be considered in personal Bible study or discussed in a classroom setting. The purpose of this book is to encourage Christians to live in such a way that reflects the hope we have for eternal life. Conversations and brainstorming around these reflections might be helpful in rekindling our passion for the church and reminding us how we should interact with each other so that when the world sees us, they see something beautiful…and different…and good.

THE HOPE PRESERVER

This is a verse about hope that appears at the end of each lesson and relates to the subject of that chapter. Reflecting on these Scriptures can help us preserve our hope, especially in times when we truly feel like shipwreck survivors just trying to hang on until rescue comes. Hope can keep us afloat when the trials and temptations of this life seem to be relentlessly pulling us down. Make these verses your Scripture focus for the week—then commit them to memory and meditate on them often.

THE MESSAGE IN A BOTTLE

At the end of every chapter, there is an opportunity to summarize your thoughts on hope and how it relates to the subject being discussed. This comes in the form of a message that you are sending out to the world in a bottle. A space is provided for you to write a few sentences in response to a chapter-specific prompt. Keep in mind that your answer is geared toward those who are looking at the church through a spyglass and who might be wondering about "a reason for the hope that is within you" (1 Pet. 3:15). Each note begins with the words, "Dear friend" and then you take over from there!

THE SEASHELLS

At the end of each odd numbered chapter, you will find an extra activity that relates to the content of that chapter. These are optional activities— kind of like seashells you might find along a shoreline— you can either pass them by or you can pick them up and take them home. If you pick up the Hope Island "seashells" when you come across them, they will enrich your spiritual life and add a bit of beauty to your study.

Come with me as we explore Hope Island...there is quite the treasure to be found!

FIRST, WE FIND WATER!

Set priorities

THE SURVIVORS

As the forty men, women, and children began to grasp the reality of their situation, it was hard not to become overwhelmed with despair. Alone on a remote island, miles from their set course, with only the supplies they could grab from their sinking ship, it was a dismal scene; except for one, perspective-changing thing: they would not be there forever. One final message had been received just as the ship was going down. The words, "Rescue is coming" had come scratching and skipping through the radio and those words had changed everything. That message gave them hope, and that hope would keep them alive.

Now, standing on the beach, the survivors brushed off the sand and began to plan. Because of their common hope, they would build a community on the island, a way of life, that would lend itself to their continued survival until rescue came.

In the first few hours spent on the island, it became clear that there were priorities that needed to be addressed in order for the survivors to continue surviving. One thought seemed to be on everyone's mind:

we have to find water. They all agreed that this task was of the greatest importance as the intense heat of the sun bore down on the island without mercy. In the lifeboats they had shared a limited supply of fresh water. That supply was now gone, leaving behind a relentless thirst and this indisputable bottom-line: without water they would die.

The captain stood in front of the group. "We need to stay hydrated. Our lives depend on it. So, our first objective is to find water. We don't know the size of this island, but there may be a source of fresh water somewhere. We'll stay together and we'll look together."

Without water, nothing else really mattered. Without water, rescue was meaningless. No water meant no life; no life meant no future; and no future meant no hope. To keep hope alive, they had to find water first. This goal would take precedence over everything else.

Before breaking through the trees that lined the beach and heading into the island jungle, the survivors gathered together in prayer. They prayed for thirst-quenching, life-giving, hope-preserving water.

THE JOURNAL

The survivors immediately set out on their quest to find a fresh water source. Shortly after making their way into the jungle, they came upon a cave nestled into the side of a rock wall. A quick inspection found the cave to be without much depth and restricted in height. As one young woman scanned the inside walls of the cave she noticed a rock that seemed out of place—sticking out a bit more than the others and awkwardly positioned. She felt the rock, wriggled it a little, and it easily slipped out from the wall. In the space uncovered there was something hidden. She reached in and pulled out a small black journal with the words, "Captain's Log" inscribed on the front. When she stepped out of the cave, the other survivors gathered around her as she opened the book and read the entry found on the first page:

Day One: Nothing matters if there is no water.

Today, our first day on this island, we found water: a fresh spring in the center of the jungle just beyond a large rock wall. For this we are grateful. I am a simple man, but I do understand the necessity of water in order to preserve life. My companions here agreed and we set out to find water with a sense of urgency that the task so deserved. We knew that without water, there would be no reason to build shelters, or make nets, or even collect food. Water was of the greatest importance. Not only would water quench our thirst, but it would also sustain us between each rise and fall of the sun.

On this island I have fostered a new relationship with water. Here, I see plainly that it has given me life. I think I shall never again cup it my hands without first whispering a prayer of gratitude for its existence.

—Paul

"And I, brethren, when I came to you, did not come with excellence of speech or of wisdom declaring to you the testimony of God. For I determined not to know anything among you except Jesus Christ and Him crucified" (1 Cor. 2:1-2).

"For me to live is Christ, and to die is gain" (Phil. 1:21).

"For there is one God, and one Mediator between God and men, the Man Christ Jesus" (1 Tim. 2:5).

THE CHURCH

First, we tell people about Jesus. In order for people to understand God's gift of salvation, they have to learn who Jesus is and what he accomplished through his death on the cross. Before people are taught about the church, how to worship, and why we need redemption, they have to know about Jesus Christ and his love for mankind. Teaching Jesus is priority, because without his sacrifice there would be no hope.

When I entered the field of nursing, I learned right away that prioritization is a key concept. In nursing school I was introduced to different strategies and guidelines for organizing tasks which I would routinely put into practice when taking care of patients in the hospital. The framework for determining priorities in nursing comes from Abraham Maslow's Hierarchy of Needs. Maslow's theory is pictured in the form of a triangle divided into categories of need, with the base category representing the needs of highest priority and the tip of the triangle representing the needs of least priority. The base of Maslow's pyramid is labeled "physiological needs," which would be those things that a person needs in order to survive—like food, water, and air. In nursing, we use the acrostic "A-B-C" when assessing a patient's basic survival needs: Airway, Breathing, and Circulation. If these three needs are not being met, then absolutely nothing else matters! Other needs, such as exercise, comfort, respect, or affection are important, but if a patient is not breathing...then those other needs are not a priority. As a nurse, you have to continually evaluate the needs of your patients so that you can be sure that the greatest needs are being addressed first.

As Christians, if we aren't careful, we can sometimes allow the most important things to become overshadowed by lesser things. It might not be appropriate to discuss issues of morality, or conversion, or various parts of worship with someone who doesn't even know who Jesus is and why he came to earth. It's not that those other topics are not important or should not be discussed—they just might not be the most effective place to start when trying to introduce someone to Christ and his church. The identity of Jesus is a fundamental truth that we must make known to the world and one that we must reflect on often so that we never take for granted the immeasurable grace of God.

Jesus Christ is the key figure in the story of man's redemption told on the pages of the Bible. He is identified throughout Scripture with a number of titles, each of them characterizing him in a unique and incomparable way. Listed below are some of those titles followed by a few Bible verses given for reference. Consider for a few moments the identity of Jesus:

Son of God

- "The beginning of the gospel of Jesus Christ, the Son of God" (Mark 1:1).

- Announced to Mary..."And the angel answered and said to her, 'The Holy Spirit will come upon you, and the power of the Highest will overshadow you; therefore, also, that Holy One who is to be born will be called the Son of God'" (Luke 1:35).

- Declared by Peter... "Simon Peter answered and said, 'You are the Christ, the Son of the Living God'" (Matt. 16:16).

- Proclaimed by God at the baptism of Jesus… "And suddenly a voice came from Heaven, saying, 'This is My beloved Son, in whom I am well pleased'" (Matt. 3:17); and his transfiguration… "While he was still speaking, behold, a bright cloud overshadowed them; and suddenly a voice came out of the cloud, saying, 'This is My beloved Son, in whom I am well pleased. Hear Him!'" (Matt. 17:5).

- "Paul, a bondservant of Jesus Christ, called to be an apostle, separated to the gospel of God which He promised before through His prophets in the Holy Scriptures, concerning His Son Jesus Christ our Lord, who was born of the seed of David according to the flesh, and declared to be the Son of God with power according to the Spirit of holiness, by the resurrection from the dead" (Rom. 1:1-4).

Savior of Mankind

- "And she will bring forth a Son and you shall call His name Jesus, for He will save His people from their sins" (Matt. 1:21).

- "For God so loved the world that He gave His only begotten Son, that whoever believes in Him should not perish, but have everlasting life. For God did not send His Son into the world to condemn the world, but that the world through Him might be saved" (John 3:16-17).

- "Then they said to the woman, 'Now we believe, not because of what you said, for we ourselves have heard Him and we know that this is indeed the Christ, the Savior of the world'" (John 4:42).

- "And I give them eternal life, and they shall never perish; neither shall anyone snatch them out of My hand. My Father, who has given them to Me, is greater than all; and no one is able to snatch them out of My Father's hand. I and My Father are one" (John 10:28-30).

- "Nor is there salvation in any other, for there is no other name under heaven given among men by which we must be saved" (Acts 4:12).

- "And we have seen and testify that the Father has sent the Son as Savior of the world" (1 John 4:14).

- "He who has the Son has life; he who does not have the Son of God does not have life" (1 John 5:12).

Founder of the Church

- "And I also say to you that you are Peter, and on this rock I will build My church, and the gates of Hades shall not prevail against it" (Matt. 16:18).

- "For no other foundation can anyone lay than that which is laid, which is Jesus Christ" (1 Cor. 3:11).

- "And He put all things under His feet, and gave Him to be head over all things to the church, which is His body, the fullness of Him who fills all in all" (Eph. 1:22-23).

Mediator and Advocate

- "Jesus said to him, 'I am the way, the truth, and the life. No one comes to the Father except through Me'" (John 14:6).

- "For there is one God and one Mediator between God and men, the Man Christ Jesus" (1 Tim. 2:5).

- "But now He has obtained a more excellent ministry, inasmuch as He is also Mediator of a better covenant, which was established on better promises" (Heb. 8:6).

- "And for this reason He is the Mediator of the new covenant, by means of death, for the redemption of the transgressions under the first covenant, that those who are called may receive the promise of the eternal inheritance" (Heb. 9:15).

- "…to Jesus the Mediator of the new covenant, and to the blood of sprinkling that speaks better things than that of Abel" (Heb. 12:24).

- "Therefore He is also able to save to the uttermost those who come to God through Him, since He always lives to make intercession for them" (Heb. 7:25).

- "My little children, these things I write to you, so that you may not sin. And if anyone sins, we have an Advocate with the Father, Jesus Christ the righteous. And He Himself is the propitiation for our sins, and not for ours only but also for the whole world" (1 John 2:1-2).

Judge

- "He who rejects Me, and does not receive My words, has that which judges him—the word that I have spoken will judge him in the last day" (John 12:48).

- "Truly, these times of ignorance God overlooked, but now commands all men everywhere to repent, because He has appointed a day on which He will judge the world in righteousness by the Man whom He has ordained. He has given assurance of this to all by raising Him from the dead" (Acts 17:30-31).

- "…In the day when God will judge the secrets of men by Jesus Christ, according to my gospel" (Rom. 2:16).

- "I charge you, therefore, before God and the Lord Jesus Christ, who will judge the living and the dead at His appearing and His kingdom" (2 Tim. 4:1).

Teacher

- Jesus was referred to and known among the people as "The Teacher" (Matt. 26:18).

- "And so it was, when Jesus had ended these sayings, that the people were astonished at His teaching, for He taught them as one having authority, and not as the scribes" (Matt. 7:28-29).

- "And He taught in their synagogues, being glorified by all" (Luke 4:15).

- "Then He got into one of the boats, which was Simon's, and asked him to put out a little from the land. And He sat down and taught the multitudes from the boat" (Luke 5:3).

- Addressed by Nicodemus as Rabbi, meaning teacher (John 3:1-2).

- Addressed by Mary as Rabboni, an endearing term for a teacher (John 20:16).

Brother and Friend

- "For whoever does the will of My Father in heaven is My brother and sister and mother" (Matt. 12:50).

- "Greater love has no one than this, than to lay down one's life for his friends" (John 15:13).

- "No longer do I call you servants, for a servant does not know what his master is doing; but I have called you friends, for all things that I heard from My Father I have made known to you" (John 15:15).

- "The Spirit Himself bears witness with our spirit that we are children of God, and if children, then heirs—heirs of God and joint heirs with Christ, if indeed we suffer with Him, that we may also be glorified together" (Rom. 8:16-17).

And More...

Lamb of God, King of kings, Lord of lords, The Word of God, The Way, The Truth, The Life, The Messiah, Immanuel, The Holy One, Shepherd, The Light of the World, The Door, The Bread of Life, Master, Son of David, Almighty, Bridegroom, Chief Cornerstone, Great High Priest, Deliverer, Author and Perfecter of Faith, Our Hope, Prophet, Redeemer, Rock, Rose of Sharon, The True Vine, The Lily of the Valley, Wonderful, Counselor, Mighty God, Everlasting Father, and Prince of Peace are just a few more of the titles that identify Jesus throughout the Bible. Knowing who he is should give deep meaning to the fact that we are able to come into a relationship with him. That relationship is realized when we do the Will of God (Matt. 12:50).

The Bible tells the story of God's love for man, man's fall to sin, and God's plan to provide a way for man to be redeemed. The hero of this story is Jesus—God's only Son and our only Savior. He is worthy. He is powerful. He is loving. He has conquered sin and death. He lives and he's coming back one day. Without him our lives would be without direction and would ultimately end in condemnation, but because of him our lives have purpose and we have hope for eternity in heaven. The world must be told about him and it's our responsibility as Christians to do the telling.

THROUGH THE SPYGLASS

Does the world see Jesus when it sees the church? Do they see Christians walking in his footsteps and living by his example? Do they see people who genuinely love and serve others? Do they see men and women who reflect the attitude of Christ in their day to day walks of life? The world must see Jesus when it sees the church! For some people, the church may be their first glimpse into who he is and how he can change their lives. We have to always be aware that our words and our actions are a representation of Christ in this world. We have a noble responsibility to shine his light and draw people to him.

There is a verse found in 2 Corinthians 2:15 that refers to Christians as the "fragrance of Christ to the saved and the perishing." A fragrance is something that lingers even when you are no longer in the presence of the one bearing the scent. Think about a pie that has been cooked in an oven and then delivered to a neighbor. The pie may be gone, but the aroma continues to fill the house. Or think about a loved one who always wears the same perfume or cologne. They may walk in and out of a room, but their scent lingers in the air long after they're gone. The same is true of Christians. Christ came into this world for just a brief time and now Christians live as his aroma in the world. It's a beautiful and honorable distinction that we have been given. When the world sees Christians, or takes in the aroma of the church, do we make them think of Jesus? It's so important that we do.

REFLECTIONS

- Who is Jesus? What makes him uniquely important to mankind?

- Why is his humanity significant?

- What aspects of his humanity can you relate to?

- What does Jesus mean to you, personally? How has he changed your life?

- The island survivors knew that without access to fresh water they would die, so finding water became a priority. Why is teaching Jesus—who he is and what he did for mankind—a priority in our Christian service?

- Is the church, as a whole, effectively teaching and preaching Jesus to the world? How about individual Christians? What are we doing right and what can we do better?

- If you were describing Jesus for the first time to someone who has never known him, what would you say?

- How would you explain to them his role in our salvation?

- Is it possible for someone to become a member of the church without bringing them to Jesus?

- In what ways do we represent Christ in our daily lives? How can we reframe our conversations and activities so that we stay Christ-centered?

- In the Hope Preserver verse below, our hope is described as "living." What is meant by a "living hope?"

HOPE PRESERVER

"Blessed be the God and Father of our Lord Jesus Christ, who according to His abundant mercy has begotten us again to a living hope through the resurrection of Jesus Christ from the dead" (1 Pet. 1:3).

MESSAGE IN A BOTTLE

The main idea of this chapter is the importance of setting priorities when it comes to sharing our hope with the world. If you could write a few words to someone who is spiritually lost describing the most crucial thing they need to know concerning their salvation, what would you say?

Dear friend,

FINDING SEASHELLS

Throughout the book of John, Jesus makes a variety of "I Am" statements. Look up the Scriptures listed on the table below and write down the word, or words, Jesus uses to describe himself. Then write down the meaning behind those descriptions and what they reveal to us about the gospel.

Scripture	I AM...	Meaning
John 6:35		
John 8:12		
John 10:9		
John 10:11		
John 11:25-26		
John 14:6		
John 15:5		

CHAPTER 2

DISCOVER AND EXPLORE!

Grow in knowledge

THE JOURNAL

Day Two: There is much to learn.

Where am I? What am I to eat? How will I withstand the dangers of this unfamiliar place? How will I survive? It is not enough that I desire rescue, although I crave it with every fiber of my being. I must live until I am found, yet I do not even know how to live in this place. But I will come to know! I will uncover the secrets of this island, and I will come to know its pleasures and its pain. I will not be zealous for rescue while starving underneath the shade of a tree whose hidden fruit might sustain me. I will not look longingly to the comfort of tomorrow while burning without shelter under the rays of the sun today.

I must be vigilant to uncover the truth about where I am and how I must live. Some things are not what they seem as I discovered before sundown on my first day in this place. I should be most careful to remain aware of my surroundings and to test those things that appear helpful, but that may in fact bring me harm.

—Paul

"Brethren, my heart's desire and prayer to God for Israel is that they may be saved. For I bear them witness that they have a zeal for God, but not according to knowledge. For they being ignorant of God's righteousness, and seeking to establish their own righteousness, have not submitted to the righteousness of God" (Rom. 10:1-3).

"For this reason we also, since the day we heard it, do not cease to pray for you, and to ask that you may be filled with the knowledge of His will in all wisdom and spiritual understanding" (Col. 1:9).

"O Timothy! Guard what was committed to your trust, avoiding the profane and idle babbling and contradictions of what is falsely called knowledge—by professing it some have strayed concerning the faith. Grace be with you. Amen" (1 Tim. 6:20-21).

THE SURVIVORS

For the survivors of the shipwreck, discovering that rescue was coming changed everything. They would be saved! Knowing this, they had reason to persevere and motivation to work together as they waited for that day. This truth would affect how they would live from day to day, how they would overcome challenges, how they would make decisions, and how they would treat each other. To discover there was rescue in the future was to discover there was purpose in the present.

Fresh water had been found just beyond the large rock wall as the hidden journal had indicated; and it not only refreshed the bodies of the survivors, it completely refreshed their souls. It gave substance to their hope. Also, the surprise finding of the journal had lifted their spirits and renewed their confidence in the future. Someone had been in their place and had shared his story! The unknown writer had made it home and his words of wisdom would help them make it home, too. They would refer to the journal daily—every morning when they came together as a group—to read the words of a former hope-filled survivor named Paul.

There was much to be done. They needed to further explore the island. This would be their temporary home and they needed to become familiar with all that it had to offer. What could they find to eat? What could they use to build a shelter? Was it truly deserted? They had to learn all they could about the terrain, the resources, and the dangers of the island. Sitting on the beach and confidently expecting rescue would do no good if they starved while waiting. They had to find nourishment and they had to find safety.

For the survivors on Hope Island, discovering and exploring was a matter of life and death.

THE CHURCH

"My people are destroyed for lack of knowledge" (Hos. 4:6). Those words originated from the mouth of God and were directed toward the Israelite nation, through his prophet Hosea, as the Northern Kingdom drew closer to its downfall. They had forgotten his laws, they had forgotten his promises, and at the very heart of the matter, they had forgotten who they were. This deficit of knowledge would lead to their rejection by God and ultimately their judgment.

Over a thousand years before God spoke those words to Hosea, he had made a promise to Abraham—a promise to make him a great nation, to give his descendants the land of Canaan, and to bless all nations through his seed (Gen. 12:1-3, 7; 13:14-17; 15:1-21; 22:15-19). Hundreds of years before God declared, "My people are destroyed for lack of knowledge," he had delivered his law to Moses on Mount Sinai and had expected the Israelites to know it, to live it, and to teach it to their children. But, looking down at the divided kingdom with its corrupt kings and unfaithful citizens, God found a people who no longer knew. He found a people who had forgotten.

The Israelites could not be a nation of hope without knowing God, without understanding his purpose, and without living according to his will. They could not confidently expect a future of blessings and fulfilled promises without knowing why or how those good things would come. God's expectation for his people is the same today: to grow in knowledge.

I'll never forget the morning that my oldest daughter walked into the kitchen where I was enjoying my first cup of coffee for the day and presented me with a proposition that began with these words, "Mom, since I'm eight years old and pretty much know everything I need to know, I was wondering if I could…" I can't even remember what she asked me because it took me some time to process the "I pretty much know everything" statement. Bless her heart for thinking that at eight years old she had it all figured out! Evie has since discovered that her capacity to learn and to grow is limitless, and that no one ever reaches a point of "knowing it all," physically or spiritually.

The value of spiritual knowledge must not be underestimated. We should never stop discovering and exploring the truths in God's Word. It's a continual process and necessary for our survival on this earth. Without knowledge, we can't be confident in what lies ahead. We can't look forward to something we know nothing about. Knowledge builds confidence and confidence builds hope.

Knowledge and Salvation

Simply stated: We cannot benefit from God's plan for our redemption if we don't know what it is. God has gifted us with the whole story—a story that begins before "the beginning." It's a story with an eternal purpose that was set into motion before Adam was formed from the dust on the ground. It's the most beautiful story ever told, about the love of a father that cannot be comprehended, and his gracious gift that cannot be measured. It's the story of man's salvation found in Jesus Christ—the most important story one could ever know.

This story is found in the Word of God: our source of truth and ultimately our freedom (2 Tim. 2:15; John 8:32). According to James 1:21, the implanted word is able to save souls, and Paul explained to Timothy that the Holy Scriptures were able to make him wise for salvation through faith in Jesus Christ (2 Tim. 3:15). Everything that we need to know for our salvation can be found in the Bible. We must read it in order to discover what God has planned and prepared for his people. Bible study cannot simply be a side-note on our spiritual journey. It's essential to setting us on course toward our eternal destination.

Knowledge and Understanding

Our journey through this life is not always easy. The road we travel does not promise to be free of pot-holes, construction delays, and unexpected closures. We are faced with choices and trials that test our faith and bring us to our knees in despair. We may wonder about our direction and whether we are making the right decisions for ourselves and for our families. Sometimes we might want to look up to heaven and cry out to God, "What should I do? Where should I go? What do you want from me?"

God has given us the answers. He has mapped our route to heaven and has lighted our path with his Word (Psa. 119:105). We've not been left in this world to figure everything out on our own. Remember the words of Jeremiah, "O Lord, I know the way of man is not in himself; it is not in man who walks to direct his own steps" (Jer. 10:23). It's a matter of trust. We have to trust God with all of our heart and not depend on our own understanding as we daily walk in this life. If we recognize him as our authority and obey him, then he will guide us in the direction that we should go (Prov. 3:5-6). God guides us through his Word and his Word directs us toward heaven. He breathed-out the Scriptures that we find on the pages of our Bibles, and his words equip us completely for all that we need in this life (2 Tim. 3:16-17). To receive God's guidance and to understand the direction he wants for us to go, we have to explore his Word.

Knowledge and Nourishment

Spiritual growth is in direct proportion to one's knowledge of the Word and the application of that knowledge in life. Our preoccupation should be with who we are and who we are becoming spiritually. Paul referred to this spiritual aspect of one's self as the "inward man." He told the church at Corinth that our outward man (the flesh) is perishing but the inward man (the spirit) is being renewed day by day (2 Cor. 4:16-18). This eternal part of you and me, the spiritual part, requires care and attention. How are we strengthening it? What are we feeding it?

The Word of God is our spiritual food and the more we feast on it, the stronger we become. As we move from the milk of the Word to the meat of the Word (Heb. 5:12-14) and our knowledge of spiritual principles deepens and broadens, an amazing thing happens to our hope. It multiplies! It intensifies! The more we learn about the nature of our God and his eternal purpose accomplished through Jesus Christ, the more we will long to be with him who loves us so completely, and the more we will yearn for Christ to come again.

One morning in our Sunday morning Bible class we were discussing spiritual growth and development. The teacher asked the question, "What do you do in order to continue growing and maturing as a Christian?" Several comments were made, but then he directed the question specifically to the oldest member of our congregation. A beautiful and wise, white-haired sister with a thin, quiet voice answered, "I read my Bible, and every time I read my Bible I learn something new." I found out later that she had read her Bible cover-to-cover countless times, and although she has left this world, I continue to hear her words: "every time I learn something new." THAT is an example of growing in knowledge! THAT is the picture of a nourished and renewed spirit, not contained by a perishing physical body!

Knowledge and Protection

Knowledge of God's Word also prepares us for spiritual battles. His Word is our sword. Truth, righteousness, faith, salvation, and the gospel represent different components of our armor (Eph. 6:10-18). When faced with spiritual warfare, we are not armed and we are not protected if we lack knowledge. We will not stand ready to fight if we've never opened our arsenal. The devil does not show mercy and he does not play fair. His fiery darts are aimed at the young, the old, the weak, the strong, the new Christian, and the life-long faithful Christian; and he knows he doesn't have much time (Rev. 12:12).

When Jesus was fasting in the wilderness just before beginning his ministry, he showed us how to use the Word to counter the devil's advances (Matt. 4:1-11). Each time Jesus was presented with a temptation, he responded with a Scripture. After three attempts, the Bible says that the devil left him. With our feet firmly planted in the Word, our shield held fast, and sword in hand, we can also resist the devil. And when we do…he'll run (James 4:7).

Knowledge is not only needed for our spiritual defense (1 Pet. 3:15), it's also needed as we fight for our faith (Jude 3). Knowledge can provide us with spiritual healing and comfort when we are suffering, and it can shelter us as we endure the storms we are sure to face in this life. To benefit from the protection God's Word offers, it is necessary for us to know what is written on its pages.

Knowledge and Judgment

One day will be "the last day," and we need to be ready! Judgment *is* coming. But we don't have to be fearful because Jesus has already told us by what standard we will be judged when that day comes. Hear his words in John 12:28, "He who rejects Me, and does not receive My words, has that which judges him—the word that I have spoken will judge him in the last day." We have in our hands the Book that contains the very words that we will have to face again when Jesus comes back. This should propel us into Bible study with a fervent desire to learn everything we can about

God's will for mankind.

When the last day comes, there will be no excuse for lack of knowledge. In Acts 17:30-31 we read, "Truly, these times of ignorance God overlooked, but now commands all men everywhere to repent, because He has appointed a day on which He will judge the world in righteousness by the Man whom He has ordained. He has given assurance of this to all by raising Him from the dead." We have the opportunity in this life, right now, to discover and explore the Word of God: to learn it and to live it. One day it will be too late!

The good news is that the more we "grow in the grace and knowledge of our Lord and Savior Jesus Christ" as Peter encouraged the early Christians to do in 2 Peter 3:18, the more we will understand and appreciate the love of God and the more we will mature in our love for God and our fellow man. As our love is perfected, fear is cast away so that we may have boldness in the day of judgment (1 John 4:18). This is a beautiful truth, and it begins with knowledge.

THROUGH THE SPYGLASS

When the world looks at the church, they should see people who are actively learning and teaching. They should see a people who encourage spiritual growth and development. They should see a people who know who they are and know where they are going. Outsiders looking in should find men and women who love to explore the Bible—excavators who dig deep in the Word to discover the truth!

They should see Bible-reading Christians who set aside time to spend in study of Scripture, who find joy in soaking up every detail found on the pages of the greatest story ever told. They should see a group of people who love the Bible, who share its message, and who regard its existence with humility and gratitude.

The world should see people who aren't afraid to discuss Scriptures; who are ready to give a defense to anyone who asks about the hope they have in way that is gentle and reverent (1 Pet. 3:15). They should see people who are confident about their faith and who are eager to talk to them about Jesus.

Most importantly, when the world sees the church, they should see people striving daily to live what the Bible teaches. They should see people who aren't perfect, but who really love the Lord and faithfully follow him. When the world looks through a spyglass at the church, let's pray that they see people who know the truth and who are reaching out with open arms to share it.

REFLECTIONS

- Where does spiritual knowledge come from?

- The island survivors considered discovering and exploring "a matter of life and death." Do you think the same is true when it comes to discovering and exploring God's Word? Why or why not?

- What do you think is the most important thing that someone who is spiritually lost should know? How do they acquire that knowledge? What do you think is the most important thing for a Christian to know? How do they acquire that knowledge?

- Knowledge of God is more than just being aware of his existence; it's a deep appreciation for who he is and the relationship that we can have with him. How do we develop that type of knowledge?

- Is it possible to have too much knowledge when it comes to spiritual matters? (Consider/Contrast 1 Cor. 8:1 and 2 Tim. 3:7 with Prov. 1:7 and Prov. 18:15).

- Can knowledge be a detriment? If so, in what way?

- Personal Bible study is one way that we can grow in knowledge of God's Word. What are some other reliable tools we can use when it comes to discovering and exploring the truth?

- Why is it important for the world to see Christians actively and openly studying the Bible?

- In what ways are you sharing your spiritual knowledge with fellow Christians? How are you sharing it with others who are not in the church?

- If the hope we read about in the Bible is defined as "a confident expectation, or a happy anticipation," explain how knowledge affects our hope? Relate this to the phrase "I hope in Your Word" found in the "Hope Preserver" verse below.

HOPE PRESERVER

"You are my hiding place and my shield; I hope in Your Word" (Psa. 119:114).

MESSAGE IN A BOTTLE

The main idea of this chapter is the importance of growing in our knowledge of God's Word. If you had to briefly explain to someone, in just a few words, how Bible reading and Bible study affect your hope, what would you say?

Dear friend,

CHAPTER 3

ONE FOR ALL AND ALL FOR ONE!

Be Unified

THE JOURNAL

Day Three: We must be one.

I am not alone here. There are others who survived the shipwreck, and we are with one another in this place until the day of our deliverance. When that day will be, we cannot know; nevertheless, at this time we must stand together for the reason of life and for the welfare of all. Today we are not from different lands, with different tongues, and different creeds; we are one. Division will surely break us. We will have to be patient with one another, humble, and kind. We will need to find a way to speak to one another, reach common resolutions, and make consistent judgments. I expect this effort will not be easy, but I am certain that our unity will promote a spirit of peace on this island.

Two days ago, as we crawled onto the sand, I prayed that self-will was left in the water. I prayed for submissive and loving hearts in its stead. I continue to pray that through eyes of grace we will each see—not man and woman, young or old, rich or poor—but that we will see one family, sharing the same joy and the same hope.

—Paul

"There is neither Jew nor Greek, there is neither slave nor free, there is neither male nor female; for you are all one in Christ Jesus" (Gal. 3:28).

"I, therefore, the prisoner of the Lord, beseech you to walk worthy of the calling with which you were called, with all lowliness and gentleness, with long suffering, bearing with one another in love, endeavoring to keep the unity of the Spirit in the bond of peace. There is one body and one Spirit, just as you were called in one hope of your calling; one Lord, one faith, one baptism; one God and Father of all, who is above all, and through all, and in you all" (Eph. 4:1-6).

"Therefore if there is any consolation in Christ, if any comfort of love, if any fellowship of the Spirit, if any affection and mercy, fulfill my joy by being likeminded, having the same love, being of one accord, of one mind" (Phil. 2:2).

THE SURVIVORS

As the captain moved his eyes from face to face, he was amazed at the diversity of the group. Different ages, different cultures, different personalities, different backgrounds, each one harboring unique regrets and ambitions. But there was one sure thing they shared in common: they were all survivors on an island looking forward to rescue.

They would have to stand together on that truth in order to survive. They could not be divided. Division would bring disaster. The captain had seen it happen before on his ship. A crew must be unified. They can't be in disagreement about where they're going or how they're supposed to get there. They can't argue over how to steer the ship or which way is north. They have to agree on their direction and they have to use the same map; otherwise, they will find themselves drifting off course, making no progress toward their destination, and certainly not enjoying the ride. If a crew cannot find one-ness, it will never find the full measure of its greatness.

As the words read from the old journal that morning played over and over in his head, the captain knew the same principle would be true for survival on the island. The survivors would have to work with each other, they would have to hold tight to what they knew to be true, they would have to lay their differences aside, and they would have to be unified. The captain stood tall and said these words to the people standing around him:

"We survived the shipwreck, came through the water, and now we are on this island. We are not going to die here. We are going home. We're going to rally around the message, 'Rescue is coming,' and we're going to help each other live to see that day. From this moment on, we are a family—a team. If one falls down, we'll pick him up; and if one gets lost, we'll search until we find her. From this moment on, we're in this together! All for one and one for all!"

Then he led them all in a prayer for unity.

THE CHURCH

As his final hours on this earth drew closer, Jesus spent time in prayer. We know from the accounts found in Matthew and Luke that our Savior was in anguish and in sorrow. Luke describes the sweat from Jesus falling to the ground like "great drops of blood" and how he knelt before God and asked, "Father, if it is Your will, take this cup away from me; nevertheless not My will, but Yours, be done" (Luke 22:41-44). Jesus despised the shame of the cross, but he endured it for the joy that was set before him (Heb. 12:2).

In John 17, we are given more details on the prayer that Jesus spoke to God. Before the end of his life, his thoughts were on his disciples, present and future. His appeal was for their protection from evil and for their unity. Listen to the words of Jesus in John 17:20-23:

"I do not pray for these alone, but also for those who will believe in Me through their word; that they all may be one as You, Father, are in Me, and I in You; that they also may be one in Us, that the world may believe that You sent me. And the glory which You gave Me I have given them, that they may be one just as We are one; I in them, and You in Me, that they may be made perfect in one, and that the world may know that You have sent Me, and have loved them as You have loved Me."

The one-ness of believers was on the heart of Jesus as he prepared to return to his Father.

Why Unity?

Unity should be important to Christians because it was important to

Jesus. He not only prayed for unity in his final hours before going to the cross, he also taught it during his time of ministry. In the book of John, he refers to himself as "the good shepherd" and in 10:16, Jesus says, "And other sheep I have which are not of this fold; them also I must bring, and they will hear my voice; and there will be one flock and one shepherd." Jesus foretold of the gospel being brought to the Gentiles and his desire for them to be welcomed into the fold, where they also would be his sheep and he would be their shepherd. A unified flock under the care of the one and only shepherd.

Unity should be important to Christians because it was important in the apostle Paul's inspired writings. Paul often encouraged the early Christians to be like-minded and to avoid division. He wrote frequently about the one-ness that is found in Christ and the peace that comes from being joined together in his body. Listen to the words found in his letter to the Ephesians (2:14-22):

"For He Himself is our peace, who has made both one, and has broken down the middle wall of separation, having abolished in His flesh the enmity, that is, the law of commandments contained in ordinances, so as to create in Himself one new man from the two, thus making peace, and that He might reconcile them both to God in one body through the cross, thereby putting to death the enmity."

Unity should be important to Christians because it has been made possible by means of Jesus Christ's death on the cross, in which God's eternal purpose reached fulfillment (Eph. 3:8-11). Thanks be to God that you and I can be fellow-heirs, of the same body, and partakers of God's promise in Christ through the gospel (Eph. 3:6)!

In the words of David, a man whose heart belonged completely to God, "Behold, how good and how pleasant it is for brothers to dwell together in unity" (Psa. 133:1).

What is Unity?

When our children were younger, they used to love to crawl into bed with me and Sam. Early in the morning, or in the middle of the night if they had a bad dream, their little bodies would nestle down between us where they felt safe and completely loved. One night, as a toddler, Evie was snuggled in close to us when she happily announced, "Look at us! We're like a puzzle—we fit together perfectly!" Since then, I've thought about those words when I think about the "one-ness" of Christians. Even though we each represent different pieces, we fit together perfectly, creating a beautiful picture of unity.

To better understand unity, we should turn to the Bible and discover how the Holy Spirit has defined what it means to be "perfect in one" (John 17:23). In 1 Corinthians 1:10, Paul pleads with the Christians in Corinth to "speak the same thing, to not be divided, and to be joined together in the same mind and the same judgment." In his letter to the church at Philippi, he encourages them to "stand fast in one spirit, with one mind, striving together for the faith of the gospel" (Phil. 1:27). In the same verse, he describes this type of conduct as being "worthy of the gospel of Christ."

In these passages we can see that unity involves the following:

- Speaking the same thing

- No divisions

- One mind

- One judgment

- One spirit

In order to have agreement on all of those areas, there must be a standard! We all must build on the same foundation, follow the same guidelines, and refer to the same source for determining what is right and what is wrong. We have to stand on the same truth! And the truth, according to John 17:17, is the holy, precious, and incorruptible Word of God.

Unity is based on truth. We cannot be unified if we don't stand together on the Word of God. If we all were to allow the Bible to guide our speech, our minds, our judgments, and our spiritual lives, the result would be a unified body of people working together in love and in peace to reach our heavenly home. And the church would grow...by leaps and bounds.

What is Not Unity?

We should be careful to have a clear understanding of what unity is, and also of what it is not. The world cries out for unity, but teaches something quite different from the biblical principle. It is important to realize that unity is not the same thing as union. "Union" carries with it the idea of being "joined together," but just because two people, or two groups of people, are "joined together" does not mean that they have unity.

Unity is also not simply "agreeing to disagree," although this is something we often hear in the world. It's not the attitude of "I'm okay; you're okay." In other words, unity is not saying "I'll do whatever I think is right and you do whatever you think is right, and we'll just get along with each other." While that might diminish conflict, while it might feel really good, and while it might be easy, we have to understand that it is not unity; at least it's not the unity that we read about in our Bibles.

Unity is based on truth. We cannot be unified if we don't stand together on the Word of God.

How Do We Get Unity?

It's possible for us to be unified! Jesus would not have prayed for something that his church could never attain. We can have unity when we all put aside our own doctrines and our own desires and hold up the Bible as our only standard of truth. We can have unity when we all follow the biblical pattern and when we all obey the teachings of Christ without adding anything to them or taking anything away (2 John 9-11; Rev. 22:19).

Unity can only be achieved on the basis of truth. In his prayer recorded in John 17, Jesus prayed for his disciples and then, in verse 20, he also prays for "those who believe in Me through their word." "Their word," refers to the spoken and written testimony of the disciples given by inspiration of the Holy Spirit and eternally preserved as the books of the New Testament (1 Thess. 2:13; 2 Pet. 1:20-21). Jesus' prayer was for those who believe, through their word, to be unified. When the Bible is our guide, and we all commit to reading it, studying it, and obeying it, then we will be a unified church. If we stand firm on the truth, practice grace and mercy, and let love be the motivation in everything we say and do, then unity will follow.

Why Do We Need Unity?

We need unity because Jesus wants his church to be unified. But why? Why is unity so important to our Lord and Savior? He tells us the reason in the prayer he lifted up to his father just before his arrest in the garden. Jesus prayed for the one-ness of believers "that the world may believe that You sent Me" (John 17:21). We are to be unified as a testimony to the world that Jesus Christ is the Son of God and was sent to the earth that through his sacrifice we can have the hope of salvation.

When Christians, together, testify to the gospel of Christ (1 Cor. 15:1-

4), the world will listen. Imagine the influence, the power, the good that would come from believers uniting on the Word of God and taking to heart the mission to "go into all the world!" The church would explode with growth! If the world were to see followers of Jesus come together in unity, putting aside all petty disagreements and man-made creeds, and lifting up the Bible as the only authority, people would listen.

We need unity because it provides the basis for fellowship. Depending on the context, the word "fellowship" in the New Testament can be defined as "sharing in common; holding a mutual interest; mutual activity; a partnership with each other; or participating together." God has called us, through the gospel, into fellowship with his Son (1 Cor. 1:9). If we walk in the light, we maintain our fellowship with deity and have fellowship with other Christians (1 John 1:5-7). To "walk in the light" is to live according to the truth, something we won't do perfectly, but that we can do faithfully. We should be liberal in extending our kindness and forgiveness to each other as we all try our best to do this daily. To enjoy the blessing of spiritual fellowship, we have to be walking in the same truth, united in one faith.

THROUGH THE SPYGLASS

When the world looks at the church, they should see unity. They should see a group of people who uphold the same truth and as a result, speak with the same mind and the same mouth. Our message should be the same! We should be striving in one spirit for the faith of the gospel. The world should not see division or chaos, which sends a message that Christianity is confusing and inconsistent. If the world sees factions and denominations, then how are they to believe in a God of order and purpose? We have to point them to the Bible where they can find everything they need to know about the church and the role she plays in God's redemption of mankind.

If we all stand on the Word of God, then we will be standing together. If we all use the Bible as our standard in everything that we do, then we will find the unity for which Jesus prayed. When the world sees the church, they should see people who are likeminded toward one another and who glorify God with one mouth and one mind (Rom. 15:5-6).

REFLECTIONS

- At the beginning of the chapter, the captain described why it is necessary to have unity among a ship's crew. Read his reflection again. How do his thoughts relate to unity in the church? On what should we, as Christians, base our unity?

- Do you think unity in the church is something that can be achieved? Why or why not? What would need to happen in order for unity to exist among believers?

- The captain made the statement: "If a crew cannot find one-ness, it will never find the full measure of its greatness." Do you think the same is true of the church? Explain your reasoning.

- What can you do, as an individual member, to promote unity in the church?

- Are there matters on which we can disagree? Are there matters on which there is no compromise? How do we determine what those matters are?

- What is the result of division in the body of Christ?

- What attitudes must Christians cultivate in order to have unity in the church?

- How does agape love influence unity?

- In Philippians 2:1-4, Paul writes to Christians about behaviors they should avoid in order to maintain like-mindedness. What are some of those behaviors? How do they create disunity?

- Consider the Hope Preserver verse below. How does 1 Thessalonians 2:13-14 tell us that we are called? How does the means by which we are "called" relate to our "one hope"?

HOPE PRESERVER

"There is one body and one Spirit, just as you were called in one hope of your calling" (Eph. 4:4).

MESSAGE IN A BOTTLE

The main idea of this chapter is that people of hope strive for unity. If you wanted to write a short note to explain the relationship between unity and hope, what would you say?

FINDING SEASHELLS

Write out Psalm 133. In the NKJV, the words "good" and "pleasant" are used in the first verse to describe unity. What do those words mean? How are they different? Then, consider in the next two verses how unity is compared to "oil" and "dew" and how those words and images contribute to the meaning of the psalm.

Dear friend,

CHAPTER 4

BUILDERS, AND FISHERS, AND COOKS...OH MY!

Recognize talents and abilities

THE JOURNAL

Day Four: Everyone here is important.

With certainty I can write about the diversity among our group here on the island. I have mentioned once before the many differences we have in appearance, character, and history, but there are also differences in ability and talent, which has proven most beneficial. We have found that we all need each other and every member of our group must do his or her part to make our life here fruitful.

Where one is weak, another is strong, and where one

has no experience, another is wise. There are some here with gifts of design, others with gifts of strength, others with gifts of music, and still others with gifts of hunting and cooking. There is neither space nor time for me to mention each unique talent represented among us, but I do know that I am grateful for what each one brings to our island family. Each member makes us stronger and I see that our lives here are blessed because of it, in spite of the most difficult circumstances.

–Paul

"For by one Spirit we were all baptized into one body—whether Jews or Greeks, whether slaves or free—and have all been made to drink into one Spirit. For in fact the body is not one member but many" (1 Cor.12:13-14).

"But speaking the truth in love, may grow up in all things into Him who is the head—Christ—from whom the whole body, joined and knit together by what every joint supplies, according to the effective working by which every part does its share, causes growth of the body for the edifying of itself in love" (Eph. 4:15-16).

THE SURVIVORS

Life on the island promised to be difficult. It would take all of the survivors working together to ensure the group's survival. Each person had something to offer because each person brought their own abilities with them—their own unique gifts and talents. On the island there was a place for everyone. Everyone was needed, and everyone felt important, because they truly were.

The survivors needed to learn all they could about each other. They needed to know each other's names and faces. On the boat, they had been strangers who just happened to be enjoying the same trip, but on the island they became family. They were a team now, a group of island dwellers, a tribe with a common goal. What professions were represented in the group? What backgrounds, cultures, and experiences? What special gifts did each one have? All of this would be important in delegating tasks, solving problems, and making decisions.

The captain stood before the group. "We've been on this island for a few days now, and it's clear that we have our work cut out for us. There is a lot to do to make sure that everyone is taken care of and that everyone stays safe. We're going to have to get to know each other better so that we can determine what gifts and talents are represented here. What we read from the journal is true: We all need each other. It's going to take all of our abilities, together, to survive. Once we figure out what each person can do, no matter how big or how small, we'll assign jobs and responsibilities so that we can effectively get things done. Everyone has a place here. Everyone matters."

THE CHURCH

God has uniquely designed each one of us and has individually blessed us with different talents and abilities. In the church, when every member uses the gifts they've been given, a beautiful thing happens: the church operates as it should; and when members encourage one another to use the gifts they've been given, something else beautiful happens: the church grows as it should.

Just recently, my son taught me a great lesson about this very thing. He had made the decision to be baptized into Christ—the most important decision he'll ever make in his entire life—and Sam and I were so proud. But just days after his baptism, he said something that made me even more proud. Briggs said, "Mom, now that I'm a Christian, what can I do to help serve?" He was motivated and ready to get to work in using his abilities for Christ and for the good of others. When we, as older members, encourage that spirit of service in the hearts of young Christians, the church will grow.

The church is the body of Christ, with Christ being the head and individual members comprising the different parts of his body (Eph. 1:22-23). This is described so beautifully in 1 Corinthians 12:12-27. Paul wrote, "For as the body is one and has many members, but all the members of that one body, being many, are one body, so also is Christ" (1 Cor. 12:12). Paul continued in the text to describe the important function of each part of the human body and then related that to the members of Christ's body, the church. Each part of the body has a specific role, whether it's an eye, an ear, a hand, or a foot, and every part works together for the good of the entire body. This is as it should be with the church! Each member of the church has a specific role, and we all must rely on the skills and abilities of each member in order for the church to function as one body. The church needs every eye, every ear, every hand, and every foot! No one is of greater or lesser importance than another. We all serve in different ways, but together we are one body (Rom. 12:4-5).

All Are Worthy

We serve a good and loving God who sees the value of every single person. Everyone is worthy in the eyes of God. Everyone is important to him. Everyone has a place in his family. He knows each detail about each aspect of his creation. In fact, he knew everything about each one of us before we were even born! Look at the extraordinary words of the psalmist, David:

"For You formed my inward parts; You covered me in my mother's womb. I will praise You, for I am fearfully and wonderfully made; marvelous are Your works, and that my soul knows very well. My frame was not hidden from You, when I was made in secret, and skillfully wrought in the lowest parts of the earth. Your eyes saw my substance, being yet unformed. And in Your book they all were written, the days fashioned for me, when as yet there were none of them" (Psa. 139:13-16).

You and I are worthy! Not because of anything we've done, but because of the love of our heavenly Father. He was aware of us, and forming us, and anticipating us, before we ever took a breath. You and I are worthy! Not because we deserve it, but because Jesus Christ is worthy and he paid the price for our eternal salvation (John 3:16).

Just as the body recognizes the worth of its parts, so the church should recognize the worth of each member. Paul explained this to the Christians in Corinth as he compared the church to the human body: "If the whole body were an eye, where would be the hearing? If the whole were hearing, where would be the smelling?...And the eye cannot say to the hand, 'I have no need of you,' nor again the head to the feet, 'I have no need of you.' No, much rather, those members of the body which seem to be weaker are necessary" (1 Cor. 12:17, 21-22). Regardless of size, strength, or skill—every member is valuable because every member is vital.

All Have Ability

Not only are we worthy in the eyes of God because of his love for us and the sacrifice of his son, but we also have the ability to use the gifts that he has entrusted us with for his glory. Worth and ability—with these two God-given attributes comes a great deal of responsibility. God has invested in us powerfully; what return is he receiving on his investment? In other words, how are we using the talents and gifts we've been given by God? What are we doing to honor him with those things? First Corinthians 12:18 says, "But now God has set the members, each one of them, in the body just as He pleased. And if they were all one member, where would the body be?" We should each ask ourselves the question, "What function am I serving in the body?"

The Parable of the Talents is one that is familiar to many people. Take a minute to read this story told by Jesus found in Matthew 25:14-30. This parable is packed with lessons for Christians, but consider these two specific messages that have to do with the gifts that have been given to us by God:

1. We have all been given gifts of varying degrees according to our ability

2. One day we'll give an account to God of how we managed the gifts he gave us.

We tend to read this parable and focus on the third servant, who hid his talent and produced nothing from what his master had given to him, but think for a moment about the first two servants. They invested their talents so that when the master came back he would receive a good return on what he had entrusted to both of them. The third servant was punished severely, but the other two servants were commended and rewarded! The comfort of this parable is found in the master's response to his servants who worked hard and were prepared for his return: "Well done good and faithful servant; you were faithful over a few things, I will make you ruler over many things. Enter into the joy of your lord" (Matt. 25:21).

Ultimately the spiritual take-away from this parable is that we should use whatever talents we have been given, to the best of our ability, for the glory of God. We have to keep in mind that God has given us what we need to accomplish this. He's blessed us with gifts and talents according to our ability; we just have to use them!

All Should Steward

Everything we have been given is a gift, including our talents. We are truly not owners of anything; we are simply managers who have been entrusted with the Master's goods until he comes back. This is the perspective we should have as we live our lives here on this earth. From talents, to jobs, to money, to children, to past experiences, to time, to opportunities, to relationships, to possessions, and even to the gospel, we are to demonstrate faithful stewardship of all that God has placed under our care. Remember the words found in the first verse of Psalm 24, "The earth is the Lord's, and all its fullness, the world and those who dwell therein."

All that we are and all that we have should be committed to serving God with the understanding that nothing belongs to us, not even ourselves! Our gifts and our abilities are given to us from God and should be used in ministry to others for his glory (1 Pet. 4:10-11). We have a responsibility to do this, and to do it according to God's plan and purpose. Ephesians 2:10 tells us that we are God's workmanship, created in Christ Jesus for good works. Are we using our God-given talents to walk in those good works that he has prepared for us?

For a period of time, if you were to ask my son what he wanted to be when he grows up, he would have told you, "I want to be a football preacher!" I was never completely sure what that meant, but I knew that Briggs loved football and I knew he loved God. So if being a "football preacher" was the way he could merge those two things together, then I was all for it! He talked about it with a lot of excitement, and I imagined him out on a football field passionately telling his teammates about Jesus. Briggs is talented when it comes to sports, and quite honestly, football preaching would be an area where I am quite sure he would excel. He would love it and I know he would do great things for the Lord. I sincerely hope if he ever became a "football preacher" that he would never be discouraged by his church family. I pray that if this is an area in which he chooses to serve that no one will tell him that it's silly or not needed. God uses people in wonderful ways when they use their unique gifts in his service!

Christians can help each other practice good stewardship when it comes to using the talents we've been given. Nobody should feel like his or her gifts cannot be used in the church! Look for opportunities to share with someone who is trying to find a way to serve. This might involve creative thinking and developing new strategies for building up the body and reaching the lost, but it can be done! And, most importantly, it can be done in keeping with God's Word.

All Can Shine

We haven't been given gifts and talents without purpose. We are to identify them, be grateful for them, and then use them to make a difference in the world. They should further the growth of the kingdom and represent the church in a positive way. They should be used to help people, to touch the lives of others with kindness, and to build up the body of Christ. Simply stated, our talents should benefit others, not ourselves!

God has graciously given every one a special gift and he wants us to be good stewards of that gift and use it to minister to each other (1 Pet.

4:10). When we recognize our gifts and talents, and put them to use in the service of others, it allows us to shine as lights in the world. This is not so that we can receive honor or praise for our good works, but so that God can be glorified (Matt. 5:14-16). The Bible tells us in 1 Corinthians 10:31 that "we should do all to the glory of God." This certainly includes the way that we manage the talents he has placed in our care until the day he comes to collect the return on his investment. We don't have to live in fear of that day! If we use our talents wisely and give all praise to God for our abilities and opportunities, we will shine as Christian lights and we will be ready when our Master comes home.

Everyone can shine when it comes to helping the church operate through the use of their talents, but we might need to place greater importance on identifying each other's gifts. Some Christians may be struggling to see where they fit in, or to recognize the abilities they have—we shouldn't leave them feeling helpless or unimportant! I heard a speaker tell a story once about a young man in a youth group who didn't feel like he had a special ability or talent to contribute to the church. The speaker said that there was nothing further from the truth, because that young man attended every single youth event. You could always count on his participation in anything and everything that was planned. "Your gift," the speaker told him, "is that you are always here. That isn't a small thing! You help the church through your involvement and your fellowship. That's huge!" What the speaker did in that moment was to help another Christian shine a little brighter by recognizing and validating one of his talents.

All Can Edify

Christians have been given the instruction to comfort each other and edify one another (1 Thess. 5:11). We all need this! We need to be on the giving end and on the receiving end. Living in this world is hard. It's especially hard for people who are striving not to be "of" the world. We need constant support from our brothers and sisters in Christ, and one thing we can do is build each other up by recognizing and encouraging the faithful use of our talents.

Let me challenge all of us to make it a point to tell someone when we see them using their abilities to serve. When a person takes the initiative to do something good for the church, whether it's part of the worship service or out in the community, take the time to say something about it, or even better, send him or her a note of thanks and inspiration! It makes a difference. This small act of encouragement can help other Christians find and develop their areas of strength when it comes to serving the Lord.

Christians can, and should, help each other with this important aspect of our spiritual lives. We can work together to identify strengths and skills, we can brainstorm ways to serve others with those abilities, and we can support each other fully as we anticipate the Master's words, "Well done my good and faithful servant!"

THROUGH THE SPYGLASS

When the world looks through the spyglass at the church, they should see a place where they can belong. They should see a place where they can use their talents and abilities, a place where they will be needed. If the church is perceived as an elite club, where only certain types of people are welcomed, then we're going to lose a lot of souls over self-righteousness and hypocrisy. We must find ways for all people to use the gifts they have been given in service to God, and it can most certainly be done without compromising God's Word. We might have to be creative and brainstorm ways we can use someone's special talent to bring people to Jesus, but God will open doors of opportunity—and his doors will never contradict what he has already revealed in Scripture.

We all have unique abilities. We can all find a special way to serve in the kingdom of God. When the world sees the church, they should see a people who work together, who celebrate special talents, and who look for ways to use each other's gifts to build up the body of Christ and reach the lost in the world.

REFLECTIONS

- What talents has God given to you? What talents has he given to those in your home or in your Bible study group?

- How can we develop our talents so that they can be used in kingdom work?

- What helps us use our talents? What prevents us from using them?

- In what ways are you using your talents to serve God? What does God promise to those who use their talents well (Matt. 25:29)?

- How can we help each other identify and use our talents in the church?

- Think of someone who you believe has a unique ability and uses it for kingdom work. What does he or she do? (Write a note of thanks and encouragement for the way that they use their gift!).

- How have you benefitted specifically from the talent of another?

- In the Survivor section of this chapter, the captain ended his comments to the group by saying, "Everyone has a place here. Everyone matters." How can we encourage someone who may feel that there is no place for them to use their talent in the church?

- What do you think is the greatest gift we, as the church, have been given to steward? How are you, personally, investing and growing that gift?

- How does using our talents bring glory to God? How does it help grow the church?

HOPE PRESERVER

"We give thanks to God always for you all, making mention of you in our prayers, remembering without ceasing your work of faith, labor of love, and patience of hope in our Lord Jesus Christ in the sight of our God and Father" (1 Thess. 1:2-3).

MESSAGE IN A BOTTLE

The main idea of this chapter is that hope filled people recognize their talents and abilities and those of others. What are your thoughts? Write a brief note to someone explaining why this is an important characteristic of the church.

Dear friend,

CHAPTER 5

WE'RE NOT THE ONLY ONES HERE!

Share the message

THE JOURNAL

Day Five: Share the opportunity.

The island is not desolate. Up until now we had assumed that we were alone here, but this is not true. There are others on this island! They are peaceful and are not a danger to us. We have acquainted ourselves with them and are taking great caution to assure them that we likewise mean them no harm. They are familiar with the ways of the island and it is certain they have been here for many years. Speaking with them has proven to be a challenge, as we do not share the same language, but they are willing to try, as we are, and we have made progress.

If one day we are able to leave this place then we must share the opportunity with the people here. It is the right thing to do. Some may not desire to leave, but regardless, it seems they are unaware of a world outside the one that has been defined by the huts within their tiny village. It brings me to tears that they may live and die and never know that there is so much more. I wish to save them all.

—Paul

"For I am not ashamed of the gospel of Christ, for it is the power of God to salvation for everyone who believes, for the Jew first and also for the Greek. For in it the righteousness of God is revealed from faith to faith; as it is written, 'The just shall live by faith'" (Rom. 1:16-17).

"Brethren, my heart's desire and prayer to God for Israel is that they may be saved" (Rom. 10:1).

"How then shall they call on Him in whom they have not believed? And how shall they believe in Him of whom they have not heard? And how shall they hear without a preacher? And how shall they preach unless they are sent? As it is written, 'How beautiful are the feet of those who preach the gospel of peace, who bring glad tidings of good things!'" (Rom. 10:14-15).

THE SURVIVORS

As dusk fell on day five it ushered in a slight chill to the air, which typically was not felt until the heavens were completely dark and littered with stars. One member of the group stood up and began gathering up kindling for a fire when all of sudden a loud cry unsettled the silence.

"LOOK!!" A young woman jumped to her feet with a finger pointing toward the island's eastern sky.

A thin line of smoke way in the distance slowly spiraled its way upward from the tree tops.

The captain quickly numbered the survivors.

All forty were standing on the beach.

Not one person was missing.

So, where was the smoke coming from? Who could have started a fire?

For a moment, it was quiet. No one quite knew what to say. The words read from the journal that morning had hung heavy over the group all day and the emotions now stirring in the hearts of the survivors ranged from fear to excitement and from worry to relief.

Then, one small voice whispered the words out loud that were presently racing through everyone's mind…

"It's true. We're not the only ones here!"

Then the same small voice, a little louder, with a little more urgency, added…

"We have to find them and tell them that rescue is coming!"

THE CHURCH

"And Jesus came and spoke to them saying, 'All authority has been given to Me in heaven and on earth. Go therefore and make disciples of all the nations, baptizing them in the name of the Father and of the Son and of the Holy Spirit, teaching them to observe all things that I have commanded you; and lo, I am with you always, even to the end of the age" (Matt. 28:18-20).

"And He said to them, 'Go into all the world and preach the gospel to every creature. He who believes and is baptized will be saved; but he who does not believe will be condemned'" (Mark 16:15-16).

With those words, Jesus ascended back to heaven. His final charge before leaving this earth was for his disciples to go and make more disciples, which involved teaching his commandments, preaching the gospel, and baptizing. Then he made the eternal promise that he would always be with them. We cannot underestimate the importance of sharing the message of the gospel and bringing people to Jesus. It's a command given to all Christians everywhere, and it's a primary mission of the church.

In 2 Corinthians 4:7, Paul wrote, "But we have this treasure in earthen vessels, that the excellence of the power may be of God and not of us." If we consider the six verses leading up to this statement, it's clear that the treasure Paul is referring to is the gospel. In verse 2, it's called "the word of God;" in verse 3, it's called "our gospel;" and in verse 4, it's called "the gospel of the glory of Christ." The gospel is a treasure! It reveals the power and wisdom of God (1 Cor. 1:18-25). In Ephesians, Paul said that as a minister of the gospel he preached "the unsearchable riches of Christ" (Eph. 3:8). He also told the Christians in Rome that the gospel is "the power of God unto unto salvation" (Rom. 1:16). When we obey it, we claim our everlasting and incorruptible inheritance that is being reserved in heaven for us (1 Pet. 1:4).

The gospel is the treasure and Christians are the earthen vessels. We carry the message of the gospel within ourselves and God is depending on us to share the message with others. The early Christians went everywhere preaching the word and the church grew! The power of the message has not changed, but we might need to rekindle our passion for evangelizing so that we can speak the Word of God with boldness like they did! We are the keepers of a treasure, but not a treasure that we are meant to keep for ourselves. If we are Christians, it's because someone cared enough about our souls to give us that treasure; we have the privilege to go into the world and do the same for others.

Going Involves Motive

In order to "go," we have to have the motivation. We have to want to go! What should make us want to go out and tell people about Jesus? Different people may answer that question in different ways, but really, it all comes down to one all-embracing motive. Consider how a common thread weaves in and out of the following reasons why Christians should share the good news about Jesus.

It's already been mentioned that Jesus' last instruction to his disciples was to go and preach the gospel. This was important to Jesus and for that reason, it should be important to me and you. At the beginning of his ministry on earth, Jesus called disciples to work by his side as "fishers of men." It's a distinction that Christians today still carry. We are his fishers, casting out the gospel net throughout the world! We are also his friends, just as his disciples were while he was here on the earth, and because we are his friends, we do what he has commanded. We can be motivated to "go" because we love Jesus and he wants us to go, has told us to go, and expects us to go.

Another motivation to "go" is wrapped up in Jesus' purpose for coming to the earth. Luke 19:10 tells us that Jesus came "to seek and save that which was lost." Sin separated man from God and placed him in a lost and hopeless state. Jesus left heaven and became flesh so that he could bring hope to a world suffering in darkness. He lived perfectly so that he could die, and that by his death, man could have a way to come back to God. He provided man the opportunity to be saved! This was the will of God and Jesus lived in complete obedience to his father. The disciples assumed Jesus' mission to save the lost when he ascended up to heaven, and as followers of Jesus today, we carry the same torch! It is now our responsibility to share the message of salvation with the rest of the world. Our desire to live in obedience to God as a by-product of our love for him (1 John 5:3) is motivation for you and me to share the good news about Jesus to all of the world.

A third motivation to "go" comes from our love for our fellow-man. The Bible tells us that God wants for all men to come to repentance and to be saved (1 Tim. 2:4; 2 Pet. 3:9). This is the highest good we could want for another! This is the agape love that we are commanded to extend to everyone, even our enemies. When we tell others about what Jesus accomplished through his death on the cross, we might open a door for someone to accept God's gift of salvation. There is no greater expression of love than that.

Our motivation comes down to this: We GO because we LOVE.

Going Involves Action

To go, to teach, to preach, to tell, to send, to baptize—all require that we do something. They involve action! Taking the gospel message to the world is not a passive undertaking. It takes planning, talking, sharing, praying, studying, giving, leaving, coming, helping, growing, and much, much more, but what we must understand is that "going" calls for action.

We simply cannot do nothing.

"How beautiful upon the mountains are the feet of him who brings good news, who proclaims peace, who brings glad tidings of good things, who proclaims salvation, who says to Zion, 'Your God reigns!'" (Isa. 52:7).

"Declare His glory among the nations, His wonders among all peoples" (Psa. 96:3).

Bring! Proclaim! Declare! We must take action when it comes to sharing the message of Jesus. If you are physically unable to "go," there is still so much you can do to spread the Good News! You can help someone else "go" through your financial support or through your encouragement and prayers. You can invite people to worship or to attend a Bible class with you. You can share the story of how you became a Christian with everyone you meet. Even if you can't "go," take every opportunity you have to "tell!"

I think about how wonderful it would be if we could all maintain the heart of a child as we advance through life. I love the sincerity, the boldness, and the honesty you find in a child's heart. When it comes to expressing feelings and beliefs, they often do so without shame or fear. I was so proud when my daughter, Kate, was given an assignment in fourth grade called, "Cell-in-a-Bag." The class had been instructed to fill a bag with items from home that could represent the different parts of a cell. On the day of Kate's presentation, she reached into her bag and pulled out a Bible. "This," she said as she held the Bible up in the air, "is my nucleus. I chose a Bible because the word of God is the very center and most important part of who I am." At nine-years-old Kate might not have been able to "go" many places to spread the gospel, but she did take the opportunity to "tell" others about God's word in a simple and beautiful way.

Going Involves Teaching

"And the gospel must first be preached to all the nations" (Mark 13:10).

If we want to bring people to Christ, we have to teach them the gospel. Plain and simple. People have to know who Jesus is, why he came to earth to live as a man, what he fulfilled through his death, and the hope that he showered on mankind when he rose up out of the grave! Without knowing this, they cannot fully understand the love of God, or the joy of worship, or the power of prayer, or the necessity of obedience, or the comfort of forgiveness, or the basis of faith. It's essential that we teach Jesus!

In Paul's second letter to Timothy, he encouraged his "beloved son" to entrust faithful men with the ability to teach others (2 Tim. 2:2) and later, in that same letter, charged Timothy to "preach the Word" (2 Tim. 4:1-4). We must understand and fully appreciate that there is no salvation apart from hearing the Word. The gospel is the power of God to save (Rom. 1:16) and people cannot be saved without hearing it (Rom. 10:13-17).

To teach others, we have to know what to teach! We have to know the message of the gospel and how the Bible tells us we should respond to it. We have to be able to tell someone what it means to be in Christ and the blessings that come from that relationship. This obligates us to be Bible students, always learning and growing in our knowledge of the Word. Someone might say, "Well, I don't have enough Bible knowledge right now to teach someone confidently." That may be true, but a Christian can always tell someone his or her personal conversion story, or what Jesus has meant to his life, or why she obeyed the gospel, or about the hope he now has for eternal life. If you are Christian, you have something to teach someone who is lost because you have something that they don't. Tell them your story and then invite them to study the Bible with you. We can't get so comfortable in our Christianity that we forget the urgency of teaching the lost. We have to light the fire in our hearts and get excited about bringing people to Jesus!

Going Involves Me and You

Each Christian has the duty to "go." This is a responsibility that we have all been given. In 1 Timothy 3:15, Paul refers to the church of the living God as the "pillar and ground of the truth." You and I, as members of the church have the privilege to stand for the truth and to spread the truth. If Christians do not do this, then who will? The work of the church is only accomplished in the efforts made by each child of God. If we have a true love and concern for the lost, if we confidently believe what we read and study in the Bible concerning God's plan to save man, then how can we not be involved in the "going?"

What if you, and those you love the most, were without Christ? What if you had not been taught the truth? What if you had no idea that you were in the position of being spiritually lost for eternity? Would you want someone to share the message of the gospel with you? Would you want someone to tell you about the hope found in Jesus Christ? Of course you would! There are people in the world—people on your street and on my street—who don't have a relationship with Jesus, who don't even know him. We have to go and tell them. If not us, then who?

I'll never forget the sweet words of a young boy I met while on a mission trip in Sarchi, Costa Rica.

Our Vacation Bible School team had been invited into the local school and one of our sessions featured the story of "The Little Boy Who Shared His Lunch." After the 5000 were sent home full and the skit came to a close, we helped the children make their own baskets of fish and bread. We talked about sharing, we talked about helping people, but most importantly, we talked about Jesus. As the students lined up to return to their class, our team began straightening the room and gathering our supplies. I felt a tug on the back of my shirt and turned around to see a young boy smiling up at me.

"Hi," I said to him. "How are you?"

That's when he said those precious words that I'll never forget: "Today is the best day."

He hugged me and then ran off.

I think about that young boy in Sarchi, Costa Rica: how he sat and watched a group of strangers come into his school to tell a Bible story. I think about him raising his hand along with twenty other students to answer a question about the lesson. I think about how he decorated his basket and colored his fish. I think about him going home and telling his family all about Jesus and the little boy who shared his lunch. I think about him remembering that day as his "best day."

As Christians, we are stewards of the gospel, the very thing that has the power to save (Rom. 1:16). It is our mission, our responsibility, to go and share it with others. Some will embrace it lovingly; others will reject it entirely. For some, the day they hear the good news about Jesus will pass like any other, but for others it will be remembered as "the best day" and they will walk away touched, changed, and hungry to know more. How can you and I not go?

THROUGH THE SPYGLASS

When the world sees the church, they should see a people eager to share the good news about Jesus. The final instruction given by Jesus before he returned to heaven was for his disciples to "go into all the world and preach the gospel to every creature" (Mark 16:15). This is our greatest mission: to tell people everywhere that Jesus has provided a way for them to be saved eternally, through his life, death, and resurrection (1 Cor. 15:1-4).

We have to share the message of the Bible! We have to talk to people about the plan of redemption God put into motion before the beginning of time that came to fulfillment through the sacrifice of his son, Jesus, on the cross (Eph. 3:8-11). We have to teach people about how this gift of salvation, by the grace of God, is offered to everyone, everywhere, and that the Bible explains exactly how we accept it. We have to explain what it means to be faithful and how faith and obedience go hand-in-hand (James 2:20; Heb. 11). We have to tell people about the church, the kingdom of God, and how we are added to it when we are baptized into his son Jesus Christ (Acts 2:47; Rom. 6:1-4; Gal. 3:26-27). We have to tell them that one day Jesus is coming back and will deliver the kingdom to his Father (1 Cor. 15:24). The world needs to see the church spreading this message of hope—in truth, in love, and with confidence!

REFLECTIONS

- On the island, what was the survivors' motivation for finding the other inhabitants? What is your greatest motivation for sharing the message of the gospel with others?

- In what ways do you share your love for Jesus and hope for heaven with others day to day?

- What do think is the most effective means of spreading the gospel to the world? How about spreading the gospel to your neighbor?

- What are some of the greatest barriers you face when it comes to sharing the gospel? How can you overcome those barriers?

- If you're not able to "go" into all the world, what are some other methods you can use to bring people to Christ?

- How do you prepare to teach someone about the gospel?

- Do you consider yourself a minister of the gospel? Why or why not?

- Who is responsible for carrying out The Great Commission (Matt. 28:18-20; Mark 16:15-16)?

- How do you live your life in a way that communicates with the world that you are not ashamed of the gospel of Christ?

- In the Hope Preserver verse below, Paul refers to the "hope of the gospel." What is the hope of the gospel? How do you obtain that hope?

HOPE PRESERVER

"If indeed you continue in the faith, grounded and steadfast, and are not moved away from the hope of the gospel which you heard, which was preached to every creature under heaven, of which I, Paul, became a minister" (Col. 1:23).

MESSAGE IN A BOTTLE

The main idea of this chapter is that people of hope share the message of the gospel with the world. Write a message to the world explaining why this is paramount to who we are as the church.

FINDING SEASHELLS

When you are talking to someone about becoming a Christian, it's helpful to tell them about your own experience. When were you baptized? What made you decide to commit your life to Christ? Take some time to write out your personal conversion story and be ready to share it often with others.

Dear friend,

CHAPTER 6

WE HAVE A MAN DOWN!

Help each other

THE JOURNAL

Day Six: Everyone is helping everyone.

It is admirable—this trait that is shared by our group as a whole. It has been here since we first crawled out of the water: hands reaching down to help others stand, arms encircling another shivering survivor, some even carrying those who were too weak to walk from the ocean to the sand. This characteristic of helping each other has strengthened and grown in our days on the island, and as it has, so has our bond of love and friendship.

Yet another wonderful thing to which I have been

witness: as people here continue to help each other, joy and confidence is flourishing. There exists an understanding that no one is alone on this island. One's needs and interests are as much a concern to everyone else. There is not one here who is simply looking out for themselves. I am unsure of how to describe it sufficiently, except to call it simple goodness. And it seems to be that as goodness is shared among us, the more goodness finds ways to be shared.

—Paul

"We should do good as we have opportunity to all men, but especially to them that are of the household of faith" (Gal. 6:10).

"Let each of you look out not only for his own interests, but also for the interests of others" (Phil. 2:4).

"See that no one renders evil for evil to anyone, but always pursue what is good both for yourselves and for all" (1 Thess. 5:15).

THE SURVIVORS

"We should get back to the group as soon as we can. The rain is coming and we don't want to be stuck out here, away from the shelters, when it does."

Dark clouds had been drawing closer to the island since the early hours of the morning, the wind had been picking up, and the air was thick with the smell of coming rain. The food gatherers finished filling their woven baskets with coconuts, mangoes, and figs as the first drops began to fall.

"Alright, let's go!"

The clouds held nothing back, and the sprinkling rain quickly turned to a downpour. The gatherers began to run. As the rain fell harder, it became more difficult to see the ground in front of them. They wound their way through trees and bushes, ducking under low hanging vines and jumping over fallen branches. The beach was close and soon they could see the outline of the small huts where their friends were waiting. They were almost there!

Suddenly, a piercing scream came from the back of their group!

The youngest of the food gatherers had fallen. His foot had caught on a broken limb and twisted when he tried to yank it free. As the others ran back and circled around the boy, they could see that his ankle was already starting to swell.

Quickly, a few members of the group dropped to the ground to check the boy for any other injuries. Others picked up the fruit that had spilled from his basket and added it to their own. The rest of the group came together, held hands, and lifted his name up in prayer.

The boy was not able to bear weight on his ankle, so two men passed their baskets to other gatherers, then picked up the boy and carried him back to the huts. After they had returned safely, a physician among the group assessed the boy's ankle and then wrapped it using a sleeve donated from another survivor's shirt. One young lady volunteered to take over the boy's responsibilities until he was able to bear weight on his ankle and by the end of the afternoon, an elderly man in the group had fashioned a cane from a sturdy branch he had found in the forest.

A burden was lifted by compassionate hands that were ready and willing to help.

THE CHURCH

The greatest helper who ever lived was our Savior, Jesus Christ. His life, his mission, and his death can be collectively defined as the most generous gift ever given. He provided the ultimate help when he went to the cross and died for the sins of the world. He showed the ultimate kindness when he touched the diseased and ate with the sinners. He did the ultimate good when he rose from the grave and defeated death forever.

If we are going to be people who follow in the steps of Jesus, we should be helpers. We should be preoccupied with kindness. We should be out doing good for others. Benevolence must be one of our priorities in the church because it represents who we are and who we serve. And we can't just talk about helping. We can't just be "well-wishers." We have to be doers! In James 2:14-17 we read, "What does it profit, my brethren, if someone says he has faith but does not have works? Can faith save him? If a brother or sister is naked and destitute of daily food, and one of you says to them, 'Depart in peace, be warmed and filled,' but you do not give them the things which are needed for the body, what does it profit?"

Helping others involves doing what we can to the best of our ability to see that someone else's needs are met. Just like evangelism, it requires that we take action! By definition, to "help" means "to give or provide what is necessary to accomplish a task or satisfy a need; contribute strength or means to; render assistance to; cooperate effectively with; aid; assist; to relieve (someone) in need, sickness, pain, or distress." If we want to be helpers, we need to take our hands, our feet, our words, and our prayers and put them to work for the good of another. This is what Jesus did throughout his entire ministry, and it's what Christians should do as well.

Think about these words found in 1 John: "But whoever has this world's goods, and sees his brother in need and shuts up his heart from him, how does the love of God abide in him? My little children, let us not love in word or in tongue, but in deed and in truth" (1 John 3:17-18).

Is it possible to love God and be unconcerned with those in the world who are in need? We should have hearts that are ready and willing to help! Here are a few reasons why...

Because We Are Christians

We see time and again in Scripture the picture of our compassionate Savior. In Matthew 9:36, we read how Jesus was "moved with compassion" for the multitude because they were weary and scattered, like sheep having no shepherd." Because he had compassion for them, he offered them his help through healing and teaching. We can also read about the compassion of the early church. Their dedication to helping each other is seen in Acts 4:32-37, where the writer describes the believers as being "of one heart and one soul" and as having "all things in common." They helped each other, even to the point of selling their possessions so that they could provide for those in need. The church today should be a compassionate church!

Kate and I were driving down a street one day when we saw a man sitting by the side of the road with a sign that said, "HUNGRY." He wasn't asking for money; he simply wanted something to eat, and Kate asked me if we could go buy him some lunch. We circled through Chick-Fil-A and returned to the man with a large lemonade and a bag full of food. As Kate passed the bag through the window, he graciously accepted with the words, "God bless you." Then as he was walking away, he turned back toward our car and called out, "Are you Christians?" Kate answered, "Yes sir. We are." He smiled and said, "Yeah. I thought so." We drove off and

Kate looked at me. "Mom," she said. "I feel really good about that. It was the right thing to do."

I'm not saying that everyone has to reach out in the same way if they find themselves in a similar situation. I am saying that Christians should continually look for ways to help others, if for no other reason except that we wear the name of Christ.

Helping others is a key principle of Christianity. It's practicing selflessness. It's putting someone else's needs above our own. Reaching out to others with kindness and generosity allows us to represent Christ in ways that are personal and deeply felt. To help another person is to express our love for them, and as followers of Christ, Christians have a responsibility to do this. We are to pattern our lives after Jesus, who lived to help, died to help, and rose from the grave to help! And he continues to help as he reigns in heaven on the right hand of God, always advocating and mediating on our behalf.

Christians should also help because we have been commanded to help. It has never been God's Will for his people to go through religious motions and show no concern for the needs of others. Helping is a matter of the heart. How can someone profess to love God and have no feelings for his neighbor who is struggling in some way? How can someone eagerly accept the grace of God and in turn not extend grace to her brother or sister who is hurting? Remember the words found in Galatians 6:2, "Bear one another's burdens, and so fulfill the law of Christ." Being a helper is a good thing to do and the right thing to do.

Because Jesus Is a King and a Servant

Jesus helped people. He came to serve people. These humble actions—helping and serving—were lovingly wrapped up in his mission to "seek and save the lost." Jesus, the King, came to earth to live as a servant.

We often talk about the sacrifice he made on the cross when he suffered and died for mankind, but we sometimes forget that his entire life was a sacrifice. From the moment he left heaven, until the day of his ascension, Jesus lived a life of sacrifice and service. Much of his ministry involved encouraging his disciples to do the same. Listen to some of his words recorded in the Gospels:

- "Give to him who asks you, and from him who wants to borrow from you do not turn away" (Matt. 5:42).

- "So the people asked him, saying, 'What shall we do then?' He answered and said to them, 'He who has two tunics, let him give to him who has none; and he who has food, let him do likewise'" (Luke 3:10-11).

- "Then Jesus, looking at him, loved him, and said to him, 'One thing you lack; Go your way, sell whatever you have and give to the poor, and you will have treasure in Heaven; and come, take up the cross, and follow Me.'" (Mark 10:21).

Give and share. We have to be helpers if we're going to be cross-bearers and followers of Jesus. We are members of a royal priesthood who have been called to be the washers of feet. We can do it because Jesus, King and servant, showed us how (John 13:14-15). As with the rich young ruler in Mark 10, Jesus is looking at us, loving us, and assuring us that our reward is treasure in heaven.

Because We Serve By Serving

We help because we serve Jesus when we serve others. In Matthew 25:31-46, we read the parable of the sheep and the goats. Jesus told his disciples a story about the judgment using the picture of a shepherd separating his sheep from his goats. On the last day, there will be a separation of people. There will be those who cared for the needs of others (the sheep), who will be eternally rewarded, and those who did not (the goats), who will be eternally punished. In respect to showing kindness to others, Jesus explained that "Inasmuch as you did it to one of the least of these My brethren, you did it to me." The message of the parable is that living a life in service to others is an essential part of the Christian life. Our responsibility is clear and one day we will be held accountable for who and how we helped. In Proverbs 3:27 we read, "Do not withhold good from those to whom it is due, when it is in the power of your hand to do so."

It is the Christian's privilege to serve God by serving others. It's not something that we resent or avoid. The Bible tells us that it is a blessing! Proverbs 22:9 says, "He who has a generous eye will be blessed, for he gives of his bread to the poor." And the apostle Paul in his emotional meeting with the Ephesian elders in Acts 20:35, reminded them of Jesus' words, "It is more blessed to give than to receive."

We also teach children to be servants when they see parents, grandparents, and other church members serving. From a young age, if we involve children in serving others, then they will grow up with a natural inclination to serve because it's been a part of who they are and what their family does for as long as they can remember. I look back on my own childhood and recall my mother cooking for people, visiting the sick, opening our home to visitors, volunteering in the summer at a camp for special needs children, teaching classes, completing her nursing degree, learning sign language, and I could go on and on and on. She always found ways to serve others, and she did it humbly and willingly. In being a servant, she taught the importance of serving.

Because the World Needs Jesus

The world needs more helpers. It needs people who care. It needs the loving kindness of the church. The world needs Jesus and we can show them the goodness of Jesus by being the goodness in the world. People are crying out for help and Christians need to answer. Proverbs 21:13 says, "Whoever shuts his ears to the cry of the poor will also cry himself and not be heard." We should listen attentively and we should respond with mercy.

Have you ever thought about the fact that you have in your possession the one thing this world needs most? This dark world needs light. Jesus said, "I am the light of the world. He who follows Me shall not walk in darkness, but have the light of life" (John 8:12). It's through the lives of Christians that Jesus' light shines in the world. You have the light that the world so desperately needs! Light expels the darkness and chases away shadows; it brings clarity and a sense of direction. When you and I reach our hands out to help others, we extend a ray of light onto their path that might lead them straight to Jesus.

Because it Pleases God

When we help others, it pleases God. We are reminded in Hebrews 13:16, "But do not forget to do good and to share, for with such sacrifices, God is well pleased." We are also told that he remembers the works of love that we do for our fellow Christians in his name (Heb. 6:10). The thought of God being pleased with our actions and remembering the good things that we do is comforting and encouraging. It should motivate us to find more and more ways to help people in need. Be liberal with your giving, be liberal with your service, and be liberal with your helping, not because of what you will get in return, but because it pleases your heavenly Father.

Helping others is also a necessary expression of our faith. In James 1:27, the writer defines religion for his readers in this way, "Pure and undefiled religion before God and the Father is this: to visit orphans and widows in their trouble, and to keep oneself unspotted from the world." James does not mean that caring for the fatherless and widows is all there is to having an acceptable faith, but we cannot have pure and undefiled religion without practically living in service to others, especially those who are in need of our help. This does not only apply to widows and orphans, but also to the hungry, the poor, the elderly, the lonely, the grieving, the imprisoned, the homeless, the abused, the rejected…all who are in need of care and attention. This is pleasing to God!

God is also a rewarder of those who do good. The Bible teaches that when we lend to the poor, we are actually lending to God, and he will repay us for that deed (Prov. 19:17). But God doesn't promise to repay us just a little, he has promised to repay us more than our cup can even hold! Jesus said, in Luke 6:38, "Give, and it will be given to you: good measure, pressed down, shaken together, and running over will be put into your bosom. For with the same measure that you use, it will be measured back to you." These verses are inspiring, but our greatest motivation for helping others should simply be love. Love for God and love for others.

THROUGH THE SPYGLASS

When the world looks at the church, they should see people helping people. They should see hands that are ready and willing to serve. Some people go through life with a "what can you do for me?" mentality— happy to receive help, but a little less interested in the idea of helping others. This is not what the Christian attitude should be! Our attitude should be like Christ. He made himself of no reputation, came to this earth in the form of a servant, and remained obedient to God in all things even to the point of death on the cross (Phil. 2:5). And he did that to help you and me. If Christ would go to such a length and give up everything he had in heaven in order to serve mankind, should not Christians do the same? He is our example, and we are to follow in his steps even when it involves suffering (1 Pet. 2:25).

The Bible teaches us to bear one another burdens, to help those who are in need, to do good, and to share. We do these things, not only because we have been commanded to, but because when we do, we spread the love of Christ to others. Being good, and doing good, makes this world a better place. When the world sees the church they should see helpers—an army of Good Samaritans—who show kindness and practice servitude, because that's what Jesus would do!

REFLECTIONS

- What is your motivation for helping others?

- Think about the situation the island survivors faced in this chapter. How might the boy have felt as he was being "helped?" What affect did this entire situation have on the group as a whole? Why is it important for the church to be a community of helpers?

- Who are we to help? Are there people we should not help? If so, how do we determine who "gets help" and who doesn't?

- What do you do personally to help others? If you have a family, are you doing something together to help others in need?

- How important does Jesus think it is for us to help? (Think again about the parable of the sheep and the goats).

- How do we glorify God when we help others?

- In sickness, pain, or distress, where do you go for help? Who, or what, are your resources in times of need?

- The idea of "being a helper" is something we teach often to young children. It's a simple but profound concept. Do you think we lose our focus on this as we get older? If so, why do you think that happens?

- Why did Jesus wash his disciples' feet? What lesson was he teaching? Why did he not just speak this message? Why did he get down on the floor and demonstrate it?

- In the Hope Preserver verse below, happiness is linked to the help and hope that comes from God. How does the help we have from God relate to the hope that we have in him?

HOPE PRESERVER

"Happy is he who has the God of Jacob for his help, whose hope is in the Lord his God" (Psa. 146:5).

MESSAGE IN A BOTTLE

The main idea of this chapter is that hope filled people help each other. What do you think the relationship is between helping and hoping? Write a short note that describes their connection.

Dear friend,

CHAPTER 7

PUT OUT THAT FIRE!

Seek peace

THE JOURNAL

Day Seven: We are peacemakers.

I believe it may not be possible to live anywhere for any period of time without experiencing dissension of a sort. We are just men, after all, and often get in the way of ourselves. Here on the island we strive for peace. That is not to say that we haven't had occasions of disagreement and times of conflict, but we have tried with diligence to maintain harmony within our number. Our circumstance has given opportunity for reflection on those things that truly matter. With that reflection we have learned that some things are unworthy of dispute. Those things that do bring about contention can be reconciled with love, gentleness, and humility.

As I think about life on this island and these people who have become my family, I cannot imagine spending my days here in turmoil. We have too much to rejoice in, too much to hope for, and too much work to do to spend our time at war with one another. The shipwreck that brought us to this place has taught us that life is precarious. Pursue peace.

—Paul

"Therefore let us pursue the things which make for peace and the things by which one may edify another" (Rom. 14:19).

"Finally, brethren, farewell. Become complete. Be of good comfort, be of one mind, live in peace; and the God of love and peace will be with you" (2 Cor. 13:11).

"Flee also youthful lusts; but pursue righteousness, faith, love, peace with those who call on the Lord out of a pure heart" (2 Tim. 2:22).

THE SURVIVORS

Until now, conflict had been avoided. The captain shifted his weight from one foot to another as he stood between two frustrated survivors. "Tell me what happened."

One man began to explain. "We are the fishers today. We had planned to spend the morning in the cove where the group yesterday caught nets and nets of fish." Motioning toward the man standing in front of him, he continued, "He decided that we should go down the beach in the direction of the caves. It's a long walk and by the time we get there half the morning will be gone and there may or may not be fish there. It's a waste of time. We know the cove is a good spot. That's where we need to go."

The captain looked at the other man and waited for his response.

"I did suggest that we walk down to the caves," the second man said. "When we were there a few days ago, I noticed a lot of fish swimming in those waters. I thought it might be a good idea for us to put our nets down in that area. It's possible that we could catch more fish in even less time. It will take more time to get there, but it might be worth it."

Although they had their own opinions on the best way to meet the goal, it was evident that both men ultimately wanted the same thing—an abundant catch of fish. The captain thought for just a moment and then spoke to the men.

"I appreciate you both for wanting to provide so well for our group. You both bring up good reasons for fishing in two different places. The cove, we know, has had a large number of fish and is a short distance from here. The caves could very well have even more fish, but it's quite a walk and may take a couple of hours to get there. Can you come to an agreement? A way to make the best use of your time while guaranteeing that everyone will be fed by the end of the evening?

The second man answered first. "It might be better to get an earlier start if we're going to fish at the caves. Maybe we could go to the cove today and then tomorrow we can leave at dawn to walk to the caves. If we don't have any luck there, we'll still have time to fish somewhere else."

The two men shook hands and agreed to the plan. It took a healthy dose of humility and a gentle reminder of the bigger picture, but peace prevailed and a friendship was preserved.

THE CHURCH

Peace is always relevant. It's necessary and beneficial. It's beautiful and timeless. But peace is often misunderstood. The peace that the world seeks is not always the same as the peace that we read about in the Bible, at least not in its fullest sense. The Bible tells us to pursue peace. It tells us to live in peace and to be peacemakers.

"Blessed are the peacemakers, for they shall be called sons of God" (Matt. 5:9).

"Salt is good, but if the salt loses its flavor, how will you season it? Have salt in yourselves, and have peace with one another" (Mark 9:50).

"Pursue peace with all people, and holiness, without which no one will see the Lord" (Heb. 12:14).

"Let him turn away from evil and do good; let him seek peace and pursue it" (1 Pet. 3:11).

In the world we talk about peace between nations and neighbors. We talk about international peace and inner peace. We talk about peace in our careers and our communities. These are all important aspects of peace. But the peace of the Bible involves something far greater—it involves the peace with God that comes through Jesus Christ. This peace affects not only our present condition, but also our eternal future! It's a peace that has been intricately woven into the very fabric of our hope.

Peace in the World

Peace, as defined in the English language, means "freedom from civil disturbance, hostility, or war; enjoyment of calm, rest, harmony, and tranquility; a state of friendliness between previously estranged parties." This is the peace that most often comes to mind when we talk about the peace in this world. It represents an absence of conflict, or the effort to get along well with others, but it's a peace that usually comes with certain terms and conditions.

When I think about this definition of peace, I remember occasions when my children were much younger and how suspicious I became when the house became too tranquil. I would be working in the kitchen or folding clothes and enjoying the "absence of conflict" as the kids played nicely together in another room. But, then, as the minutes passed, and harmony seemed to be prevailing, I began to wonder if everything was truly okay. Something must be wrong. It's been too quiet for too long. One time, I was cooking dinner and this exact situation was taking place. My girls had been together in the living room playing with their princesses when I realized I hadn't heard any fussing, any giggling, or even any talking, for more than a few minutes. I called out from the kitchen, "Hey! Are you girls alright? What's going on in there?" Evie hollered back with complete honesty, "I'm just painting Kate blue." And she was. She had colored with blue marker all over Kate's body, and Kate was just letting it happen! There was an effort the girls were making to get along with each other (peace), as long as Kate was sitting still and allowing herself to be turned into a Smurf (the condition). This can be characteristic of worldly peace. The world says, "We can have peace, but only IF you do this, this, and this."

The peace that is offered by the world can depend on a person's emotions or perceptions. It's a peace that might involve compromise or surrender. It results from doing or saying the "right" thing, having the "right" job, or the "right" income. This peace can be unstable—here one day and gone the next—or always just beyond your reach.

It's sad to see what some people will do to try to find this kind of peace. They search for it in the wrong places and in the wrong people. They try to force it with power or suppression. They desperately chase it through money, status, or substance abuse. This is not what the Holy Spirit had in mind when through Peter's pen he said, "seek peace and pursue it." The root of the problem is that in the world, peace does not have to involve God. In fact, some may tell you that faith is not necessary at all in order to experience peace. But that is not what the Bible teaches. The peace that we read about in the Bible has everything to do with God and is directly related to our faith. It involves the same aspects as the world's concept of peace, but has an eternally deeper meaning.

Peace in the Bible

The peace of the Bible is enduring, limitless, and it even reaches beyond our understanding. The word "peace" is mentioned hundreds of times in Scripture. It's essential to our mission, our purpose, our joy, our relationships, and our sanctification. In order to better grasp the concept, it's helpful to look at the words most frequently translated from Hebrew and Greek to mean "peace."

In the Old Testament, the Hebrew word for peace is shalom, literally meaning "totality or completeness, including fulfillment, maturity, soundness, and wholeness." Depending on the context, shalom can also mean "health, posterity, tranquility, quiet, contentment, friendship, or the end of war." The word shalom could be used in a variety of instances because of its variety of meanings. It was frequently used as a farewell, when parting ways with someone. To bid "shalom" was not simply to wish rest or lack of conflict for someone, it was to wish for them completeness, or fulfillment. There is beautiful meaning found in that one word.

In the New Testament, the Greek word for peace is eirene, literally meaning "a joining of what has been separated; setting at one." Depending on context, eirene can also mean "security, safety, prosperity, national tranquility, quietness, rest, harmony between individuals, or the blessed state of devout and upright men after death." Biblically speaking, what has been joined that was once separated? What has been "set at one"? To answer those questions and to truly know the importance of peace, we have to go back to the beginning. We have to consider God's eternal purpose and exactly what he accomplished through his Son.

Before he spoke the world into creation, God knew that man would fall to sin. He knew that sin would separate him from man and that man would require redemption. His eternal plan involved sending his son to earth to give his life as propitiation for man's sin. Through the death of Jesus, man could be reconciled to God and have the hope of eternal life. Because of that sacrifice we have been "set at one" with God! What was once separated has been joined together! THIS is the peace that rules in the heart of the Christian! Because of Jesus, you and I can have peace.

Jesus Christ is Our Peace

"For unto us a Child is born, unto us a Son is given; and the government will be upon His shoulder. And His name will be called Wonderful, Counselor, Mighty God, Everlasting Father, *Prince of Peace*" (Isa. 9:6, emphasis added).

"Peace I leave with you, *My peace I give to you*; not as the world gives do I give to you. Let not your heart be troubled, neither let it be afraid" (John 14:27, emphasis added).

"These things I have spoken to you, *that in Me you may have peace*. In the world you will have tribulation; but be of good cheer, I have overcome the world" (John 16:33, emphasis added).

"*For He Himself is our peace*, who has made both one, and has broken down the middle wall of separation, having abolished in His flesh the enmity, that is, the law of commandments contained in ordinances, so as to create in Himself one new man from the two, *thus making peace*, and that He might reconcile them both to God in one body through the cross, thereby putting to death the enmity. And He came and preached peace to you who were afar off and to those who were near. For through Him we both have access by one Spirit to the Father" (Eph. 2:14-18, emphasis added).

We have peace with God because of Jesus, which leads to peace in our heart, which extends to peace with others. Jesus is the foundation of it all! Peace results in every area of our lives as a result of our relationship with God, made possible by Jesus Christ. Strong's Greek Lexicon sums it up nicely with these words: "For the Christian, it's the tranquil state of a soul assured of its salvation through Christ, and so fearing nothing from God and content with its earthly lot of whatsoever sort that is."

We aren't told that, as Christians, we will experience freedom from trouble, or hostility, rather we are promised peace in the midst of trouble. It's the constant reassurance that we live for something greater: that our hope is in heaven and not in this world. It's the comfort of knowing who we are and whose we are. It's the peace that we have as Christians that allows us to say, "Greater is He that is in me than he that is in the world" (1 John 4:4), and "The Lord is on my side, I will not fear. What can man do to me?" (Psa. 118:6).

It's a peace that is promised to all of God's people. It's a peace that works within us and is available to us far beyond our ability to even understand it (look at Paul!). It's a peace that is intended to be an abiding state of being, meaning that it doesn't "come and go." It's a part of who you are and it remains with you every day! This is what God wants for you and me…a heart filled with peace! And it's all because of Jesus.

Peace Begins With Faith

Two stories are told in the book of Luke about two different women. Take a moment to read those accounts found in Luke 7:36-50 and Luke 8:40-48. The first story is about a sinful woman who washed the feet of Jesus with her tears, wiped them with her hair, and anointed them with fragrant oil. Jesus used her example to teach a lesson on love and forgiveness. The last recorded words that Jesus said to the woman were, "Your faith has saved you. Go in peace."

The second story is about a woman with a physical condition that required healing. She pushed through the crowd, touched the hem of Jesus' garment, and was immediately healed. Jesus felt the power go out of him when she touched his garment and he asked the crowd, "Who touched me?" Eventually, the woman came forward and admitted that she had touched him and had been healed in that same moment. Jesus said to her, "Daughter, be of good cheer; your faith has made you well. Go in peace."

They came to Jesus in faith and left with the blessing of peace. What a lesson for us! Faith is the key! The peace that comes from God is a matter of faith. It's trusting in his power to help you, comfort you, and care for you no matter what circumstances you face. To choose peace, you must first choose faith.

To Find Peace, Find the Truth

There can be no peace without harmony in the truth. People cry out for peace in the spiritual world, but want to compromise truth to have it, and that's not possible! If people want peace, then truth must dominate.

We have to agree on a standard to which right and wrong is measured. We can't have peace if we don't have the same standard. There will be conflict, frustration, anger, and sorrow. Disunity will occur and division will result. But if there is the upholding of truth, which is the Word of God, then unity follows and there can be peace.

We have to be willing to talk to each other and listen to each other as we all do our very best to pursue truth. When she was just a little girl, I was talking to Evie about something she was not supposed to do. I stood there explaining to her why she should not do it and what the consequence would be if she did. In the middle of my lecture, Evie dramatically lifted her hands to her ears and twisted them, pretended like she removed them from her head, and then stuffed them into her back pocket. I was shocked! "Did you just take your ears off?" I asked her. She lifted her chin and turned her head just a bit and acted like she didn't hear me.

Needless to say, I removed her ears from her back pocket, secured them back to her head, (with imaginary super glue), and finished my lecture on our way to the "time-out" chair. Evie had not liked what I was saying and so she decided that she just wouldn't listen. We as Christians, if we're not careful, can have the same attitude when it comes to discussing spiritual matters. We should never "take our ears off" and ignore each other instead of listening and reasoning together. The truth will always stand; it will always prevail, and Christians should work together to support it and promote it, so that peace can abound.

Matthew Henry once said, "Peace is such a precious jewel that I would give anything for it but truth." This is a wonderful way to look at peace and truth together. Peace is precious, but nothing is worth giving up the truth. When you find the truth, take hold of it, stand on it, implant it in your heart, and when you do, you are sure to find peace.

THROUGH THE SPYGLASS

When the world looks at the church, they should see peacemakers. They should see men and women who live for something much bigger than themselves which allows them to face trouble and conflict with an eternal perspective. They should see people who are certain about where they're going and whose hope rests in heaven and not in this world. They should see people who turn away from evil in order to pursue peace (Psa. 34:14). They should see people who know who they are and whose they are, and who can proudly exclaim, "The Lord is on my side, I will not fear. What can man do to me?" (Psa. 118:6).

Christians can be peacemakers when we tell others how to access the peace that only comes from being in Christ Jesus (John 16:33). We can be peacemakers when we read and study the Word of God and then live it, so that the fruit of the Spirit will be evident in our words and in our actions (Gal. 5:22-23). We can be peacemakers when we go to God in prayer and let him know what we are grateful for and what our needs are, because he has told us that if we do that, then he will allow his peace—a peace that is beyond comprehension—to guard our hearts (Phil. 4:6-7). If we strive for peace, the world will notice, and God will be glorified!

REFLECTIONS

- How is the peace of the world different from the peace of the Bible?

- Does the promise of peace ensure that we will not experience trouble or hostility? What are we promised with the peace that comes from God?

- What relationship does truth have with peace? Is it possible to have one without the other?

- When we have peace with God through Jesus Christ, we are able to extend peace to others. What does that peace look like? Is it simply an absence of conflict? Is there more to it than that?

- Jesus said in Matthew 10:34-36 that he did not come to bring peace, but a sword. What did he mean by that? How does the fact that he is the Prince of Peace harmonize with these verses?

- How does Jesus bring us peace?

- For peace to prevail on the island, the survivors had to keep the bigger picture in mind. They had to talk and listen to each other with a spirit of humility. With that in mind, how can the church of Christ spread peace in the world today? List some ways you think this is being done and/or suggestions on how it can be done.

- Paul wrote in Romans 8:6 that to be spiritually minded is "life and peace." What does it mean to be "spiritually minded" and what does that look like in day to day living? How does that bring "life and peace?"

- Philippians 4:6-7 talks about the "peace of God guarding our hearts through Jesus Christ." In this context, what is our part in receiving that peace?

- In the Hope Preserver verse below, Jesus is described as the Hope of Israel. How is Jesus your hope in times of trouble? How does that relate to peace?

HOPE PRESERVER

"O the Hope of Israel, his Savior in time of trouble" (Jer. 14:8).

MESSAGE IN A BOTTLE

The main idea of this chapter is that Christians should be peacemakers. What does hope have to do with peace? Write down your thoughts in a short note that you'd like to send out to the world in a bottle.

FINDING SEASHELLS

Listen to the words of the song "Peace, Perfect Peace." Think about a time in your life when you deeply felt the peace that comes from God. Think about what you were experiencing in your life at that time. For some, it may have been a time of pain and suffering, and for others it may have been a time of happiness and stability. If you are in a group or a class, share your experiences with each other and discuss what they reveal about the peace we find in Jesus.

Dear friend,

CHAPTER 8

YOU CAN DO THIS!

Be encouraging

THE JOURNAL

Day Eight: Encouragement is a gift.

If there is something for which I am most grateful, besides that my life has been spared to this point, it is that I have companions with me who make this situation bearable. If I were alone, I imagine how easy it might be to allow discouragement and worry to darken my days. As it is, they still try to creep into my mind, but I am thankful that I have friends who help chase them away. My friends keep me encouraged. They build me up when my spirit is weak. They comfort me when I am troubled. I pray that I have been able to do the same for them.

It is good to have people by your side. It is good to have people you can lean on when you can't find the strength to stand. It is good to have people to remind you that difficult times will come to an eternal end. It is my wish that everyone could be surrounded by those types of people, but even more, it is my hope that everyone lives to be one. From this day forward, it will be my aim.

—Paul

"For I long to see you, that I may impart to you some spiritual gift, so that you may be established—that is, that I may be encouraged together with you by the mutual faith of both you and me" (Rom.1:12).

"We then who are strong ought to bear with the scruples of the weak, and not to please ourselves. Let each of us please his neighbor for his good, leading to edification" (Rom. 15:1-2).

"Therefore comfort each other and edify one another, just as you also are doing" (1 Thess. 5:11).

THE SURVIVORS

It had been designated a day of exploration. The survivors had already seen much of the island, but there were still areas in which they had not set foot since arriving there over one week ago. The plans had been made, food had been packed, and the group had risen early to begin what would be a long day of hiking and climbing. They set their sights on a particular mountain that could be seen from their cluster of huts along the tree line near the beach.

The walk to the mountain took the group through dense vegetation, made up mostly of tall trees with twisty vines and tangled branches. The temperature was sweltering, the air felt heavy, and the canopy of leaves above them did little to block the relentless rays of the sun.

Finally, they approached the base of the mountain. There was one last obstacle to cross before they started their upward climb: a creek. Although it was narrow, what it lacked in width was compensated by force of current. Looking up and down the river, the captain saw a place where large rocks connected bank to bank.

"We can cross here!" the captain called out. "Just a few steps on the tops of these rocks and we'll be on the other side."

One by one the survivors crossed the creek until there was only one person left. A young woman stood alone on the bank, her mind had flashed back to the days she had spent drifting in the ocean after the shipwreck, and she was frozen with fear.

"Come on over! You'll be fine!" the captain yelled.

"I'm scared!" she answered. "I..I..I'm afraid that I'll fall!"

Her island family did not hesitate. They immediately began cheering for the young woman, shouting words of comfort and encouragement. Several group members returned to the other bank, surrounded their friend, and offered her their whole-hearted support. They took her hands and stepped across the rocks with her, whispering prayers of courage until they all reached the other side, together.

THE CHURCH

Encouragement is essential within the church, and because God knows how desperately his children need it, he doesn't simply suggest it…he commands it! The following verses give just a glimpse at the importance of this beautiful Christian principle:

"Now I myself am confident concerning you, my brethren, that you also are full of goodness, filled with all knowledge, able also to *admonish one another*" (Rom. 15:14, emphasis added).

"But *exhort one another daily*, while it is called 'Today,' lest any of you be hardened through the deceitfulness of sin" (Heb. 3:13, emphasis added).

"And let us consider one another in order to stir up love and good works, not forsaking the assembling of ourselves together, as is the manner of some, but *exhorting one another*, and so much the more as you see the Day approaching" (Heb.10:24-25, emphasis added).

Encouragement can drive away feelings of despair, depression, uselessness, and loneliness. It can offer someone what they need to hear, sometimes whether they want to hear it or not! It can brighten a dark day or fill an empty cup. Encouragement is a small package of grace, wrapped in love, kindness, and wisdom, and delivered with the intention of drawing someone closer to Christ.

It's been said that encouragement is like oxygen for the church. This is such a meaningful analogy! For the human body, oxygen is life. When oxygen levels are low, the body suffers with symptoms like shortness of breath, restlessness, confusion, and elevated heart rate and blood pressure. Ultimately, without oxygen, the physical body will die. In the same way, the body of Christ will suffer if encouragement is absent or failing. It keeps our hearts steady, our minds clear, and our spirits strong. Encouragement supports the life of the church! And we need it now more than ever!

Times Are Troubling

It's not easy to live in this world. God understands that! He knows that encouragement is necessary, which is the reason that he instructed Christians to help and support each other. In the book of John, Jesus warned that "in this world you will have tribulation," then he added these comforting words, "but be of good cheer, I have overcome the world" (John 16:33). Jesus tells us to expect adversity while we're here, but then he encourages us with the reminder that he's already conquered this place!

Our world is broken. It's characterized by sin, futility, and death. It's ruled (for now) by the prince of darkness, and he has filled hearts with selfishness, guilt, despair, and hate. We live in bodies that are dying, face challenges daily, feel pressure to conform to the world's standards, and we struggle between the spirit and the flesh. But this should come as no surprise! The Bible has told us to expect a world of trouble. In 1 Peter 4:12, we are promised suffering; in 2 Timothy 3:12, we are promised persecution; and in James 1:2-3, we are promised various trials. We need encouragement, and we need it today!

If you watch the news or scroll through headlines on social media, it doesn't take long to realize that we live in a world of misguided and troubled souls. It's especially disheartening to see the trends in suicide and depression continually rising among our young people. The rate of suicide and attempted suicide is significantly higher now than ever before. Their involvement in gangs and experimentation with drugs and alcohol is an indication of deep seeded despair and hopelessness. These young men and women desperately need to feel a sense of belonging and need to know that they are valued. They need to be encouraged. They need to know that they do have purpose and they do have hope.

Depression, despair, and hopelessness are not limited to just our youth. Adults also turn to substance abuse, sexual immorality, and other self-destructive behaviors in an effort to cope with the challenges they face day to day. Discouragement may not cause us to sin, but it can make it very difficult to get out of bed in the morning or carry on throughout the day without feeling lost or defeated. The simple truth is that we all need to be encouraged. Encouragement makes it easier to live as a Christian in this fallen world.

Hearts Need Lifting

With all the trouble we are facing in the world, it comes as no surprise that hearts are in need of lifting. Thanks be to God for being our Rock, never-changing and ever faithful. Thanks be to the church for sharing a mutual faith, always edifying, supporting, and comforting one another. We have to depend on God, his Word, and our church family for strength and encouragement. You and I also have to be doing our part, individually, in the building up of others. It's a beautiful and essential way of extending grace to our brothers and sisters in Christ.

Because it concerns the condition of our hearts, it's important that we have an understanding of what encouragement is and how it's able to change perspective and reset direction. Biblical encouragement is more than just complimenting someone or doing something nice for them. That kind of encouragement is wonderful and needed because it can definitely brighten someone's day, but the encouragement that we read about in the Scriptures has an even deeper purpose.

Encouragement is shared with the intent to comfort the heart. This was the reason Paul told the Colossian church that he was sending Tychicus, "…that he may know your circumstances and comfort your hearts" (Col. 4:8). How is a heart comforted? There are countless ways! Comfort comes through the reminder of God's promises, through the counting of blessings, through the evidences of God's Providence, through the company of friends and family, through words of hope and love, and through reading and meditating on the Word of God. This type of encouragement keeps eyes focused on heaven and gives spirits the will to keep pressing on.

After a particularly rough shift at the hospital, I came home feeling really down and somewhat defeated. It was a night full of difficult situations that challenged me emotionally and mentally. I was in the kitchen telling Sam about some of the events of the night when my son walked in the room. He could immediately see that I needed serious lifting up. He stood in front of me, spread his arms wide open, and said, "Come here and get in these arms!" He wrapped me up in the biggest hug his ten-year-old self could give, and my heart was comforted. My sweet Briggs knew just what I needed!

In the New Testament we find that encouragement was a regular part of the early church's life together (Acts 13:15, 16:40, 18:27, 20:1-2, 27:36). They shared words of exhortation and comfort in order to motivate each other to continue walking in faith (Acts 14:22), hope (Rom. 15:4), unity (Col. 2:2), joy (Acts 15:31), strength (Acts 15:32), perseverance (Heb. 10:25), and with the assurance of Christ's return (1 Thess. 4:18). The church today needs to make encouragement a regular part of our ministry to each other. Without it, we might become overwhelmed and burdened. Without it, we might lose our focus and direction. Without it, we might feel alone and unloved. So, God tells us to be encouraging. Let's remind each other often that we are loved, thoroughly equipped, and treasured by God. Let's stand in front of each other when times are hard and say, "Come here and get in these arms!"

Barnabas Imitating

No other person in the New Testament illustrates the ability to encourage better than Barnabas, whose name actually means "Son of Encouragement." In Acts 4:36, we learn that he was a Levite from Cyprus with the given name of Joses (or Joseph). He was a wealthy and generous man who earned the wonderful nickname of Barnabas. Imagine what a man he must have been for the apostles to go to the extent of changing his name in honor of his ability to encourage others!

For the church to have a heart of encouragement, we each need to have a heart like Barnabas. To cultivate that type of heart there are a few lessons we can learn from his life and apply to our own. First, we should be good, full of faith, and led by the Holy Spirit through the Word of God. This is how Barnabas is described in Acts 11:24. The church recognized these qualities in him and chose him to go to Antioch to encourage the believers there. And he did! Which leads to the next lesson we learn from Barnabas: we should be excited for the cause of Christ and the spreading of the gospel. In Acts 11:23, we read that when Barnabas arrived in Antioch and witnessed the grace of God, it made him glad! He encouraged the church there telling them that "with purpose of heart they should continue with the Lord," and at the end of verse 24 we are told, "a great many people were added to the Lord." Barnabas had an amazing gift that he used for doing kingdom work! Finally, we learn from Barnabas that we should love people and not possessions. Because of Barnabas, the needs of fellow Christians were met (Acts 4:32-37). Because of Barnabas, the apostle Paul was first accepted by the church in Jerusalem (Acts 9:26-27). Because of Barnabas, Mark was given a second chance as a missionary of the gospel (Acts 15:36-39). The man known as the "Son of Encouragement" genuinely cared for people.

Barnabas loved Jesus and he loved the church. He wanted to see the church grow and he worked to help make that happen. He was a man of deep conviction and was willing to serve in whatever way the Lord wanted to use him. To the believers of his time, Barnabas was a blessing, and he continues to bless us today through his examples of encouragement.

God Is Waiting

Becoming a more encouraging person is a matter of choice. You and I can choose to have a heart like Barnabas. God is waiting! And if we make that choice, the church will grow. People want to be nurtured and supported. They want to believe that they can become stronger, happier, and purposeful, and they should see in the church that with God's help, they can!

Several years ago, in her third grade class, Kate had to select a hero to describe to her classmates. The assignment required that the students draw a picture of their hero and describe in a few words why they chose that particular person. I was so honored that Kate picked me as her hero. When she brought home her picture, I admired my portrait and was excited to see that she had written an acrostic in order to describe me using the letters M-O-M. Here is what she wrote: My hero—Only everything good—Much more kind than last year.

What?! Much more kind than last year? Kate quickly explained that what she meant was that my kindness keeps growing, but we have had some good laughs over the years about "that one year when I wasn't really kind." I share that story because written words of encouragement are meaningful. I keep every sweet note my children give to me, and I also keep every card sent to me from my sisters and brothers in Christ. People need to hear that they are appreciated and loved. It's uplifting and motivating! When I'm discouraged, I can look at that picture Kate drew, remember that I'm somebody's hero, and be inspired to act like it.

Encouragers promote conduct that produces Christ-like character!

Encouragers bring out the best in people! Encouragers support and lean on each other! And how do they accomplish these things? They listen in a way that makes people feel understood. They lift others up using the truth of God's Word, and they are patient and slow to judge. They take time for others and make them feel special. They rejoice with those who rejoice and weep with those who weep. They are sincerely happy for the personal victories of others, and they are sincerely concerned when others are struggling or hurting in any way. They speak with Proverbs 16:24 in mind, "Pleasant words are a honeycomb, sweet to the soul and healing to the bones."

God provides us with his comfort so that we might be a comfort to others. Remember these words found in 2 Corinthians 1:3-4, "Blessed be the God and Father of our Lord Jesus Christ, the Father of mercies and God of all comfort, who comforts us in all our tribulation, that we may be able to comfort those who are in any trouble, with the comfort with which we ourselves are comforted by God." Ask yourself each morning, "What can I do to lift someone's heart closer to Christ today?"

THROUGH THE SPYGLASS

When the world sees the church, they should see encouragers. They should see people building up people! They should see people comforting people! They should see Christians crying together, laughing together, hurting together, and celebrating together. When the world sees the church, they should see a group of people who stand by each other and cheer each other on through the ups and downs and twists and turns of this life. It should be an encouragement to the world to see the encouragement between Christians!

The church should be a people who provide comfort from a world of trouble. Through encouragement we can help each other live in this place until it's time for us to go Home. Those outside of the church should see that so clearly that it makes them want to be a part of it. People are looking for hope. They are desperate to find meaning in their lives, and they're looking for a reason to endure. They can find all of that in Jesus Christ, and the church must show them the way. Being encouragers can open the door. We must show the world that in the church there is support, there is strength, there is love, and there is hope!

REFLECTIONS

- Who has encouraged you recently? What did they do or say that lifted you up or comforted your heart?

- What actions can you take in order to make encouragement a daily discipline in your life?

- Who do you know that needs encouraging right now? What can you do to help?

- What Bible verse would you share with someone who needs encouragement in their faith?

- Encouragement should also be given to someone who is struggling with sin or who is making harmful choices. How can you offer encouragement in this type of situation?

- What actions did the survivors take to offer encouragement to the frightened woman? How do you think their actions affected the woman? What about the affect it had on the group as a whole? How can encouragement affect the growth of the church?

- What can we learn from the early church about encouragement? How did they use it in their ministry to each other and as an outreach to the community?

- Is being an encourager an option? Is it okay to choose not to be an encourager? Some people, like Barnabas, have the gift of encouragement. How can someone who may not be gifted in this way still practice encouragement?

- In the Hope Preserver verse below the word "comfort" is sometimes translated "encouragement." How do we gain encouragement from the Scriptures? How does that influence our hope?

- Do you have a favorite chapter or verse in the Bible that encourages you the most?

HOPE PRESERVER

"For whatever things were written before were written for our learning, that we through the patience and comfort of the Scriptures might have hope" (Rom. 15:4).

MESSAGE IN A BOTTLE

The main idea of this chapter is that hopeful people are encouraging people. Why is this true? If you could write a note describing the connection between hope and encouragement, what would that note say?

Dear friend,

CHAPTER 9

LIVING HERE IS HARD!

Expect persecution

THE JOURNAL

Day Nine: It is difficult to live here.

Some days the island shows no mercy. Some days I believe it wants me to die here. When I think I have seen the extent of its afflictions, I am taken aback by something new and often times worse. The days are long and the trials are unending. Nevertheless, I know that this can be expected of a place that is remote and largely uncivilized. I should not be surprised that I face troubles here to which I am not accustomed. I simply must press on.

Perhaps if someone should read these notes, they will find comfort in knowing that I have shared in their suffering. I have walked where they are walking and I have struggled through the same challenges. I do not know what tomorrow will bring, but I am here today to declare to the world that all of this will be worth it when I find myself in the tender embrace of home.

—Paul

"The Spirit Himself bears witness with our spirit that we are children of God, and if children, then heirs—heirs of God and joint heirs with Christ, if indeed we suffer with Him, that we may also be glorified together. For I consider that the sufferings of this present time are not worthy to be compared with the glory which shall be revealed in us" (Rom. 8:16-18).

"And we labor, working with our own hands. Being reviled, we bless; being persecuted, we endure; being defamed, we entreat. We have been made as the filth of the world, the offscouring of all things until now" (1 Cor. 4:12).

"Yes, and all who desire to live godly in Christ Jesus will suffer persecution" (2 Tim. 3:12).

THE SURVIVORS

To this point, life on Hope Island may sound perfect. There's unity, a sense of belonging, people helping people, peace prevailing; but life on the island was anything but perfect. Every day brought new challenges and no one was exempt from trial and suffering. If a survivor had not yet faced a trial, the question was not, "Will she?" the question was "When will she?" Life on the island was never easy.

The captain took a mental note: "There has been a snake bite, a sunburn, a rash on someone from an unknown source, and an animal has stolen the stash of fruit that was supposed to feed the group for the remainder of the day. All of this since day break, and the sun is just now at its highest point. There are many hours to go before night fall."

It was hard not to feel discouraged. It was hard not to let the ferocity of the island break their spirits and diminish their joy. They had to remind themselves often that the island was not their home. They had to remember that the island never promised them luxury; it was not a place of rest and security. They could count on life being difficult there. They had to talk to each other about the good they had found in each other and how happy they were to not be alone. They often shared their gratitude for the journal that had been found their first day on the island. It gave them comfort to know that others had walked the same beaches and gathered food from the same trees and prayed under the same sky.

Today marked the ninth day with no indication of how much longer they would remain there. In the meantime, life on the island continued, with each day ushering in new hardships for the survivors.

But they had each other. And they had hope.

THE CHURCH

In 1578, an extraordinary accidental discovery was made just north of
Rome on a road known as the Via Salaria: an entrance into the ancient
catacombs! Since that time archaeologists have uncovered many more of
these underground burial sites which have provided us with a fascinating
glimpse into our Christian history. The catacombs of Rome have been
dated from the first to third centuries, and evidence suggests that they
might have been used as late as the fifth century. The images found on
the walls of the rooms and tunnels indicate that some of these burial sites
were used by Christians, including courageous martyrs who suffered and
died for their faith.

One of the images frequently etched into the walls of the Roman
catacombs was an anchor. The anchor was an early Christian symbol used
to represent the hope found in Christ that extends beyond this life of pain
and persecution: an appropriate inscription for the walls of a Christian
tomb. It's possible that this symbol derived its meaning from the Hebrew
epistle believed to have been written sometime in the 60s AD, prior to the
destruction of Jerusalem in 70 AD. Under the order of Emperor Nero,
the open persecution of Christians was in full effect and the words of
Hebrews 6:17-20 must have given them fortitude in the face of fear:

"Thus God, determining to show more abundantly to the heirs of
promise the immutability of His counsel, confirmed it by an oath, that
by two immutable things, in which it is impossible for God to lie, we
might have strong consolation, who have fled for refuge to lay hold of
the hope set before us. This hope we have as an anchor of the soul, both
sure and steadfast, and which enters the Presence behind the veil, where
the forerunner has entered for us, even Jesus, having become High Priest
forever according to the order of Melchizedek. "

Hope: an anchor of the soul. This picture of hope was meaningful to
the early Christians who endured very real and very horrific persecution.

Hope kept their eyes focused on heaven. Hope reminded them that pain and suffering in this life are temporary. Hope grounded them and strengthened them when fear tried its hardest to destroy their faith. Hope won. It still wins. Every. Single. Time. Hope is always stronger than fear.

Remember, We Aren't Promised "Easy"

There is no promise given to Christians that the road they walk in this life will be easy. In fact, the very opposite is true. In the Bible we read that we are promised persecution: "Yes, and all who desire to live godly in Christ Jesus will suffer persecution" (2 Tim. 3:12). We are sure to be hated: "Do not marvel, my brethren, if the world hates you" (1 John 3:13). We are to expect affliction: "We are afflicted in every way, but not crushed; perplexed, but not driven to despair; persecuted, but not forsaken; struck down, but not destroyed; always carrying in the body the death of Jesus, so that the life of Jesus may also be manifested in our bodies. For we who live are always being given over to death for Jesus' sake, so that the life of Jesus also may be manifested in our mortal flesh. So death is at work in us, but life in you" (2 Cor. 4:8-12).

My mom's mother was a beautiful and wise Christian woman. She lived as a preacher's wife for many, many years and touched countless people with her knowledge of the Bible and her kind spirit. She was a strong woman, with lots of spunk, and an unwavering love for the Lord. As she neared the end of her life, her final days were spent at home surrounded by her children. During that time, she often repeated these words, "I hope my family will stay strong. I hope my family will stay strong for what's coming."

I am not sure what my grandmother believed would be coming, but I do know that her desire was for her children, grandchildren, and great-grandchildren to faithfully endure the trials of this life so that we might enjoy a marvelous reunion in heaven one day. Granny was an incredible blessing to our family while she was here on this earth and she continues to bless us and encourage us through the echo of her final words: "Stay strong."

A difficult life is what a Christian should anticipate! This does not mean a life of despair or defeat. We are never forgotten or abandoned! But a life of hardship? Yes. A life of persecution? Absolutely. The apostle Peter told Christians not to be surprised when we are tested with certain trials, as if something strange is happening to us. He challenged us to rejoice when we share in the sufferings of Christ and when we're insulted because of him, because God is glorified through us and our reward is gladness and blessing (1 Pet. 4:12-14).

But then, why did Jesus tell us in Matthew 11:28-30 that he offers us rest? Didn't he say that his yoke is easy and his burden is light? He does offer rest. He offers eternal rest and the peace that comes in knowing that we have been brought back to God when we had been separated by sin. His yoke is easy and his burden is light because Jesus has paid the price for our redemption. We don't have to try to earn God's favor. We never could if we tried. Through his sacrifice on the cross, Jesus lifted the burden of sin from our shoulders and offered us the hope of salvation. When we accept that gift of grace, we choose the abundant life...not the easy life. We choose a life of faithful obedience which involves effort, growth, change, and trial. But if you've chosen this life, you've chosen well, because you've chosen a life that ends in victory and eternity.

Remember, Jesus Walked the Same Road

We should think about Jesus often. One reason, among many, is because of his empathy. He understands us completely. He knows what it's like to live in our world: he's faced the devil's deceptions, he's suffered at the hands of others, and he's been hated and ridiculed unjustly. The Bible tells us that Jesus was tempted in every way that we are, and although he never sinned, he does sympathize with our weaknesses (Heb. 4:15). Jesus understands the persecutions that we face here on earth. If we continue reading in the fourth chapter of Hebrews, the writer tells us that because we have a sympathetic High Priest, we can come boldly to the throne of grace so that we can receive mercy and grace in our time of need (Heb. 4:16). This thought can bring us comfort when we feel like we are alone facing giants of adversity. Jesus understands, because he has been there.

Jesus can understand our loneliness because he has felt alone. He can understand our hunger because he has been hungry. He can understand our grief because he has grieved. He can understand our pain because he has been in pain. He can understand our feelings about death, about rejection, and about sorrow because he has experienced them. He understands it all because he has walked this same road we are on. And in a precious demonstration of his compassion, Jesus did not leave his empathy behind when he left this world and ascended to heaven; instead, he carried it with him where he sits on the right hand of God today, sympathizing with us in our humanity. He hears us cry out "My spirit is willing but my flesh is so weak!" and he understands.

When weariness and discouragement try to push their way into our souls, we should remember the hostility that Jesus endured from sinners (Heb. 12:3) and hold onto the hope that we have because he went to the cross. We have a perfect example in Jesus, who suffered the worst persecution, and his footsteps extend infinitely before us that we might follow him all the way Home.

"For to this you were called, because Christ also suffered for us, leaving us an example, that you should follow His steps: 'Who committed no sin, nor was deceit found in His mouth;' who, when He was reviled, did not revile in return; when He suffered, He did not threaten, but committed

Himself to Him who judges righteously; who Himself bore our sins in His own body on the tree, that we, having died to sins, might live for righteousness—by whose stripes you were healed" (1 Pet. 2:21-24).

Remember, Choose Praise

When we face persecution, it's good to think about Job. His story reminds us that there are two ways we can respond to God in our times of trial: we can curse him or we can praise him. In Job 2:9-10 we find Job being rebuked by his wife during his suffering: "Then his wife said to him, 'Do you still hold fast to your integrity? Curse God and die!' But he said to her, 'You speak as one of the foolish women speaks. Shall we indeed accept good from God, and shall we not accept adversity?' In all this Job did not sin with his lips." Job chose to praise God in his trials and ultimately God blessed him with more than he had before. Many hundreds of years later, James, the brother of Jesus, remembered how God worked in the life of faithful Job, and wrote, "Indeed we count them blessed who endure. You have heard of the perseverance of Job and seen the end intended by the Lord—that the Lord is very compassionate and merciful" (James 5:11). God's people will face trials, but if we choose praise, God will rain his blessings down on us just as he did for his servant Job.

Trials contribute to the building of a Christ-like character, which in turn builds our hope. Think for a moment about what Paul wrote in Romans 5:3-4, "And not only that, but we also glory in tribulations, knowing that tribulation produces perseverance; and perseverance, character; and character, hope." And also the words found in James 1:2-4, "My brethren, count it all joy when you fall into various trials, knowing that the testing of your faith produces patience. But let patience have its perfect work, that you may be perfect and complete, lacking nothing." The word "perseverance" and the word "patience" in both of these verses are translated from the Greek word *hupomone*, which is defined as "endurance, steadfastness, or a patient waiting for." It literally means "to remain under" as in one's ability to "remain (or endure) under" the challenges she faces in life. As trials produce this perseverance, the image of Christ that is being made in us becomes clearer and clearer, and our joyous anticipation of heaven grows greater and greater. We can praise God in times of trial knowing that there is a perfect and complete work being produced within us.

Trials make us spiritually stronger. This was something that the apostle Paul believed wholeheartedly. He recognized that his outward man was in a perpetual state of dying while his inner man was growing stronger with every criticism, every struggle, and every grief. He knew that in his weakness, he would ultimately find strength; not because of any special ability of his own, but because God had begun a good work in him and was carrying it on to completion (Phil. 1:6). Paul trusted in that and he became a man who could praise God in trials. In his letter to the Corinthians, Paul wrote, "And He said to me, 'My grace is sufficient for you, for My strength is made perfect in weakness.' Therefore most gladly I will rather boast in my infirmities, that the power of Christ may rest upon me. Therefore, I take pleasure in infirmities, in reproaches, in needs, in persecutions, in distresses, for Christ's sake. For when I am weak, then I am strong" (2 Cor. 12:9-10). He encouraged his readers with these words, "Therefore we do not lose heart. Even though our outward man is perishing, yet the inward man is being renewed day by day. For our light affliction, which is but for a moment, is working for us a far more exceeding and eternal weight of glory, while we do not look at the things which are seen, but at the things which are not seen. For the things which are seen are temporary, but the things which are not seen are eternal" (2 Cor. 4:16-18).

Trials also remind us that we need God and that he will help us. God looks at his children and says, "Call upon Me in the day of trouble; I will deliver you and you shall glorify Me" (Psa. 50:15). God wants us to come to him with our needs and desires. He wants us to cry out to him when we feel discouraged or burdened. We should remember the urging of the Hebrew writer who said, "Let us therefore come boldly to the throne of grace, that we may obtain mercy and find grace to help in time of need" (Heb. 4:16). God wants to hear our prayers and stands ready to pour his mercy and grace upon his children. He is a good and loving Father who has promised to give us the strength that we need in whatever situation we face. Paul found this to be true and he discovered true contentment. "Not that I speak in regard to need, for I have learned in whatever state I am, to be content: I know how to be abased, and I know how to abound. Everywhere and in all things I have learned both to be full and to be hungry, both to abound and to suffer need. I can do all things through Christ who strengthens me" (Phil. 4:11-13). Whatever this life places in our paths, we must remember that God is not against us—he is on our side—upholding, renewing, and comforting us always.

Remember, You Are Not Alone

As we encounter persecutions in this life, no matter how great or small, it's important to remember that we are not alone. We have the promise from God that he will never leave us or forsake us (Heb. 13:5), and we also have the company of fellow Christians. As members of the body of Christ, we support each other and help each other. We bear each other's burdens (Gal. 6:2), and when one suffers, we all suffer with her (1 Cor. 12:26)! This is what the church does! We love each other through pain, illness, and loss just as we love each other through happiness, health, and success.

The devil is working hard to keep us from eternal life in heaven, and he knows that it's easier to attack people when they are weak and alone. Christians have to stand together. We have to completely surround those who are feeling beaten down physically, emotionally, mentally, or spiritually. We have to stop allowing each other to struggle silently and separately. All over the earth there are Christian men and women who are suffering at the hands of evil. In 1 Peter 5:8-9 we are warned, "Be sober, be vigilant; because your adversary the devil walks about like a roaring lion, seeking whom he may devour. Resist him, steadfast in the faith, knowing that the same sufferings are experienced by your brotherhood in the world." Christians everywhere need to know that they are not alone. We are in this together. We have to resist and remain steadfast in the faith together.

Remember, Heaven Will Be Worth it All

We're on to bigger and better things! Remember that! We are pilgrims who are "just a passin' through." The things of this earth will one day be gone and when they are, we will be somewhere else claiming our incorruptible, undefiled, and never fading inheritance (1 Pet. 1:4). We have to adopt the mindset of Paul, when he said, "For to me, to live is Christ, and to die is gain" (Phil. 1:21). While we are here in this world, our focus is Jesus Christ—and with focus will come great blessing, but also great trial. We must endure, knowing that death brings reward for the faithful Christian. Heaven will be worth every bit of suffering that we face in this life! That is a God-given promise we read in Matthew 5:10-12. "Blessed are those who are persecuted for righteousness' sake, for theirs is the kingdom of Heaven. Blessed are you when they revile and persecute you, and say all kinds of evil against you falsely for My name's sake. Rejoice and be exceedingly glad, for great is your reward in Heaven, for so they persecuted the prophets who were before you."

We are promised that if we are hated for the sake of Christ, but endure until the end—we will be saved and we will reign with him (Matt. 10:22; 2 Tim. 2:11-12). We are promised that nothing we face in this life can separate us from the love of Christ and ultimately we are conquerors over every evil thing, because of him who loved us so immeasurably (Rom. 8:35-37). We are promised salvation (1 Pet. 1:9), eternal life (1 John 2:25), and a crown of life if we are faithful until death (Rev. 2:10).

Our hope—our confident expectation—is that the best is yet to come. The trials and afflictions of this life are preparing us for "a far more exceeding and eternal weight of glory" (2 Cor. 4:16-18). We can't even imagine what lies ahead, but we can know that it will be worth anything and everything we face here.

THROUGH THE SPYGLASS

When the world sees the church, do they see people who choose to do the will of God and not man, even if it results in persecution? Do they see people who endure persecution because they refuse to compromise their faith? They should! They should see people who hold on so strongly to their hope that they are not shaken by adversity. They should see people who are willing to suffer for doing good when it's according to God's will.

Polycarp, a student of the apostle John, is remembered for his leadership in the early church and his martyrdom in 155 A.D. He was revered as a teacher and for his diligence in upholding the teachings of the apostles. At eighty-six years old, Polycarp was arrested by Roman officials for his devotion to Christ, and ordered to appear before the local proconsul. He was told that he must recant his faith, proclaim, "Caesar is Lord" and offer incense to a statue of Caesar. Polycarp refused and made this bold statement, "Eighty and six years have I now served Christ, and he has never done me the least wrong: How then can I blaspheme my King and my Savior?" His sentence was handed to him—he was to be burned at the stake. Although the details of his death differ slightly, one thing is certain: Polycarp never denied Christ and never renounced his faith even as the flames were rising. People were watching, witnesses heard his words, and historians recorded the events. In Polycarp, and in all of the brave martyrs who were persecuted to the point of death, hope prevailed! When the world sees Christians, they should see people who patiently endure hardship and who rejoice that they are counted worthy to suffer shame for the name Christ.

REFLECTIONS

• How is hope an anchor of the soul? Where does our anchor hold (Heb. 6:17-20)?

• Do you agree or disagree that hope is stronger than fear? Explain your thoughts.

• How can Jesus promise us rest and a "light burden," but at the same time promise us tribulation and suffering?

• Why is it so important that Jesus understands and sympathizes with our weaknesses? How does this contribute to his role as our Advocate?

• How have some of the trials you have faced led to opportunities to shine the light of Christ? What doors were opened for you to grow or glorify God during a time of difficulty?

• The challenges and troubles the survivors encountered on the island are related to the trials and sufferings experienced by Christians. What persecutions do Christians face today globally? Nationally? In your community? What trials have you faced because of your faith?

• Do you think outwardly expressing Christianity will ever be prohibited in our country? Why or why not?

- Have you ever been ridiculed, rejected, or punished in some way because of your faith? How did you respond? How did it affect you spiritually?

- Why should we glory or be joyful in tribulations? And how do we do that?

- In the Hope Preserver verse below, the spiritual helmet worn by the Christian is the hope of salvation. What is significant about this piece of armor representing hope?

HOPE PRESERVER

"But let us who are of the day be sober, putting on the breastplate of faith and love, and as a helmet the hope of salvation" (1 Thess. 5:8).

MESSAGE IN A BOTTLE

The main idea of this chapter is that people of hope will face persecution. It's true that the world is a difficult place in which to live. Describe to someone, in a few words, why hope is of the greatest importance when faced with trials or suffering.

Dear friend,

FINDING SEASHELLS

The Word of God strengthens us and sustains us. It helps us endure trials and withstand temptations. The importance of knowing God's Word and keeping it hidden in our hearts is immeasurable. Let me encourage you to devote time to memorizing Scripture. This week, buy a pack of spiral bound index cards. Begin by writing down the Scriptures you've already committed to memory – one per card. Then, add new Scriptures regularly, reading them over and over until you can recite them without looking. Take these index cards with you when you go out and look through them often. Just remember: it's not enough to simply memorize the Scriptures...you also have to live them!

CHAPTER 10

QUITTING IS NOT AN OPTION!

Don't give up

THE JOURNAL

Day Ten: Keep pressing on!

Whatever happens, I will not give up. Right now, I have committed to this course upon which I have been placed and I will not quit. I remind myself often of what I am hoping for and I hold onto that hope with all of my heart. These days are hard, yes, but I am stronger today than I was yesterday. On this island I am faced with something new each day, but as a result, I learn something new each day. I must remember that the work I am doing is not fruitless. I have not been defeated! I am surviving!

I tell myself again and again that this island is not where my story ends. When challenges arise, I decide first that I will not be overtaken by them, and then I fight—fight—fight! I run from the things that would fill me with bitterness, fear, and anger, and chase after those things that bring me joy. I will not lose heart...because I have already won!

—Paul

"I press toward the goal for the prize of the upward call of God in Christ Jesus" (Phil. 3:14).

"But you, O man of God, flee these things and pursue righteousness, godliness, faith, love, patience, gentleness. Fight the good fight of faith, lay hold on eternal life, to which you were also called and have confessed the good confession in the presence of many witnesses" (1 Tim. 6:11-12).

"Therefore I endure all things for the sake of the elect, that they also may obtain the salvation which is in Christ Jesus with eternal glory. This is a faithful saying: 'For if we died with Him, we shall also live with Him. If we endure, we shall also reign with Him. If we deny Him, He also will deny us. If we are faithless, He remains faithful; He cannot deny Himself'" (2 Tim. 2:10-13).

THE SURVIVORS

The tenth day started like all the others. There was food to gather, huts to maintain, washing to be done, nets to be repaired, and wood to be collected. Every one woke up early to begin their work before the heat of the sun became unbearable.

Each person had a responsibility, either on their own or with a small group. One of those groups had the task of checking the huts and reinforcing them as necessary due to the island's daily wear-and-tear. As one man carefully tried to remove a section of a roof to replace with a sturdier one, he lost his balance and fell forward into the side of the hut. The force of his fall caused the entire shelter to collapse beneath him. It would take all day, and many hands, to reconstruct.

The man yelled out in frustration. "That's it! I've had enough! I'm done. Completely done." He turned his back to the ocean and opened his arms to the island. "You win. Alright? Do you hear me? You.Win." He dropped to his knees in the sand and held his head in his hands. His whole body shook with the cries that came from deep within his chest.

His shouts of anger turned quickly to whispers of defeat. "I can't keep going. I just can't. Maybe the message was wrong. Maybe this is where it ends."

The captain ran over to the man and sat down next to him in the sand. Other survivors came and stood in a circle around the two men. "I understand how you feel," the captain began. "I believe we all do. I know that you're tired. I know you're discouraged. But, I need you to understand this: Quitting is not an option. You have to keep going. You can't give up, because rescue is coming."

Arms reached out from the circle and touched their friend and a prayer for strength and perseverance was offered. And everyone's heart was lifted.

THE CHURCH

We were not meant for failure! From the words "In the beginning" to the final "Amen" the truth that rings from the pages of the Bible is that if we are children of God in Christ Jesus…we WIN! We are already victorious! Jesus has already conquered death, the fate of the deceiver is already sure, and a crown of life already awaits the faithful Christian. These are things that we can know! This is why we have hope!

You and I are a part of the greatest story of love and redemption ever written, but it's up to us whether we will live for the hero or the enemy. If we live for Jesus and follow the will of God, then we will enjoy the happiest of eternal endings. If we deny Jesus and allow Satan to rule our hearts, then our end is darkness and eternal death. We get to choose. God gave mankind freewill and we can choose whether or not we will accept his gift of grace through faith and live in obedience to him, or not. He has a will for us, but it's our decision to follow it.

When we accept God's gift of grace and enter into a relationship with Jesus Christ through baptism, we decide to live a new life. We no longer live according to the flesh, but according to the spirit. That means our minds aren't set on things in the world; our minds are set on spiritual things—kingdom things—things that transform us more and more into the image of Christ. Satan doesn't make it easy. The flesh wars against the spirit and the spirit against the flesh, a dilemma that led Paul to cry out in Romans 7:24, "O wretched man that I am! Who will deliver me from this body of death?" It's difficult, this conflict between the flesh and the spirit, and that's why we've been issued special armor to wear into battle. This God-given armor, described in Ephesians 6, helps us to stand against the devil and fight the good fight of faith.

We have to remember who we are. We are good soldiers of Jesus Christ! We endure hardship, we don't become entangled in matters of the world, and we live in a way that is pleasing to the one who enlisted us (2 Tim.

2:3-4). With Jesus, we are on the winning side, but we have to remain faithful to him until the very end. We can't quit after one skirmish! Christianity is for life! Keep going—even when you want to give up— because quitting is the only sure way to lose.

Christianity: A Lifelong Race

When we decide to live according to God's will, we are embarking on a lifelong commitment. We are stepping out onto a road that will wind through the remainder of our time on this earth. This road rolls over mountains and down into valleys; it takes us along steep cliffs and across rickety bridges. It's a hard road with abrupt turns and unexpected pot holes, but it's also a splendid road that promises breathtaking scenery, unforgettable experiences, and exceptional company.

This lifelong commitment that we enter when we become Christians has been compared to a race. But it's not just any race; we've signed up for a marathon! This means that we don't set out with the intent of dropping out after the first mile or two, or when the running becomes difficult. We set out knowing that finishing the race is a matter of endurance. It will take effort to run the hills and motivation to stay the course! We will need to remain disciplined and focused. The writer of Hebrews described it this way, "Therefore we also, since we are surrounded by so great a cloud of witnesses, let us lay aside every weight, and the sin which so easily ensnares us, and let us run with endurance the race that is set before us" (Heb. 12:1).

Keep in mind, that this race is not a competition with other Christians. We are individual runners and have different paces, different strengths, and different weaknesses. We are all at unique places in our growing faith and shouldn't look at other runners to compare ourselves spiritually. One day we will each give an account of ourselves to God (Rom. 14:12), and it won't matter how anyone else ran the race! You and I are responsible for the things we do in our bodies—good and bad (2 Cor. 5:10). There is no one else responsible for me, but me, and no one responsible for you, but you! Let's not become discouraged by the speed or endurance of others. Just be happy that they are on the course! Cheer them on, learn from their wisdom, or ask them for help. Instead of competing against fellow Christians, we can focus on encouraging the struggling runners, training new runners, and strengthening our own faith so that we can be the best runners we can be. The only one we're trying to beat is the devil!

A word of caution: There is a sense of urgency in this race. Unless Jesus appears in the air during our lifetime, we have an appointment with death. We don't know when it will be, but we know that we aren't promised tomorrow. James tells us that in James 4:14, and goes on to say that life is a vapor that "appears for a little time and then vanishes away." We have to keep running so that we can cross the finish line, whether that will be today, tomorrow, or years from now.

Choose to Run

The first thing to know about the Christian race is that we have to choose to be in it! We have to decide to be a runner! This is a matter of faithful obedience to God and humble acceptance of his grace. It all begins with hearing the truth about Jesus Christ—who he is and what he accomplished through his life on this earth, his cruel death, and his glorious resurrection. If we truly believe that Jesus is the Son of God and that through his sacrifice we can have the hope of eternal life, we should be motivated to take action! The Bible tells us to confess the name of Jesus, to repent of our sins, and to be baptized into Jesus so that our sins can be forgiven and removed. We choose to be a runner in the Christian race when we choose to faithfully obey God.

"*I have chosen the way of truth*; Your judgments I have laid before me. I cling to Your testimonies; O Lord, do not put me to shame! I will run the course of Your commandments, for You shall enlarge my heart" (Psa. 119: 30, emphasis added).

"Let Your hand become my help. For *I have chosen Your precepts*" (Psa.119: 173, emphasis added).

Baptism is the beginning of this race—the starting point of the marathon. What follows is a life dedicated to Christ. We won't live perfectly, but we can live faithfully! When we stumble or when we fall, we just get back up and keep running. That's a choice we make. Every morning, before we place our feet on the floor to begin our day—we choose to run.

Stay the Course

There are some things we can know from the Bible that can help us remain faithful race runners. The first thing we should remember is that to follow the course is to follow the will of God. There are two aspects to God's will: his sovereignty and his commands. His sovereign will cannot be broken. It's God's complete power over all things, and it will come to pass. Daniel wrote, "He does according to His will in the army of heaven and among the inhabitants of the earth. No one can restrain His hand of say to Him, 'What have You done?'" (Dan. 4:35). In Ephesians, Paul described God's sovereign will in this way, "In Him also we have obtained an inheritance, being predestined according to the purpose of Him who works all things according to the counsel of His will" (Eph. 1:11).

The other aspect of God's will involves our obedience and can be broken. When you and I disobey God or fail to keep his commandments, we are not following his will. His will is also described in the Bible as his judgments, his precepts, his word, his law, his statutes, his testimonies, and his ways. In Psalm 119, David beautifully wrote about the joy and blessings that come from following the will of God. We are wise to understand what God's will is (Eph. 5:17). It was Jesus who said, "Not everyone who says to Me, 'Lord, Lord,' shall enter the kingdom of heaven, but he who does the will of My Father in heaven" (Matt. 7:21). God's will has been revealed completely to us in Scripture. We can know it, we can live it, and it will lead us in the right direction. To be a faithful race runner and to stay the course, we have to make his will, our will. "For you have need of endurance, so that after you have done the will of God, you may receive the promise" (Heb. 10:36).

To remain faithful runners, remember that God gives us strength. He is our help. The Almighty Creator of the universe stands ready to help us! That's both humbling and empowering. When you struggle with staying the course, rely on the strength of your heavenly Father. "I will lift up my eyes to the hills—from whence comes my help? My help comes from the Lord, who made heaven and earth. He will not allow your foot to be moved; He who keeps you will not slumber" (Psa. 121:1-3). How blessed we are to have an eternal source of strength and comfort! "Blessed is the man whose strength is in You, whose heart is set on pilgrimage" (Psa. 84:5; cf. Psa. 29:11; 46:1; 73:26; Isa. 40:29; Eph. 6:10).

To stay the course, we also have to put our trust in God. The Bible tells us that God establishes our steps (Psa. 37:23) and directs our paths (Prov. 3:5-6), but we have to trust him and commit ourselves to doing his will. "Delight yourself also in the Lord, and He shall give you the desires of your heart. Commit your way to the Lord, trust also in Him, and He shall bring it to pass" (Psa. 37:4-6; cf. Psa. 28:7; Isa. 26:3; Jer. 17:7-8).

Don't forget to lean on others. It's easier to stay the course when you have people supporting you and cheering you on. We should be present in each other's lives and helping each other when the running is difficult. There are going to be times in your life when the only way you are able to keep moving forward is by putting your weight on your brothers and sisters in Christ and allowing them to help you along. That's what God's family does for each other! "As iron sharpens iron, so a man sharpens the countenance of a friend" (Prov. 27:17). (Also, Prov. 11:14; James 5:16).

Run to Win

We are in this race to win and that's exactly how we should live. Paul said in 1 Corinthians 9:24, "Do you not know that those who run in a race all run, but one receives the prize? Run in such a way that you may obtain it." We are supposed to run to win the prize, but the good news about the Christian race is that there's a prize for everyone who finishes. There isn't going to be just one winner! Everyone who remains faithful until the end will receive the crown of life (Rev. 2:10).

As the apostle Paul neared the end of his life, his sight was set on the finish line. Sitting there in a Roman prison, anticipating his death, Paul was ready. In the last letter he wrote, Paul said to his dear friend Timothy, "I have fought the good fight, I have finished the race, I have kept the faith. Finally, there is laid up for me the crown of righteousness, which the Lord, the righteous Judge, will give to me on that Day, and not to me only but also to all who have loved his appearing" (2 Tim. 4:7-8). Paul had been in the race to win it, and he was fully confident that because of his faith, there would be a crown waiting for him.

When Paul became a Christian, he made it a point to do exactly what Hebrews 12:1 tells us to do in order to run the race with endurance: he laid aside every weight and ensnaring sin. He didn't allow adversity or threats to throw him off course, and he didn't count his life "dear to himself" as he told the Ephesian elders in Acts 20:22-24. He focused on the race and specifically on his ministry to spread the gospel of God's grace. This was his mission: to dedicate his life to Christ. Paul had a past that surely made his race difficult. He had been a persecutor of

Christians! He was the self-proclaimed "chief of sinners!" But he kept running. He stayed in the race. In his letter to the church in Philippi, he wrote, "Brethren, I do not count myself to have apprehended; but one thing I do, forgetting those things which are behind and reaching forward to those things which are ahead, I press toward the goal for the prize of the upward call of God in Christ Jesus" (Phil. 3:12-14).

Throughout my childhood, my family had a motto, of sorts. We never actually called it our "motto," but it was a phrase that we used frequently, and I believe it accurately represents the spirit of our family. My dad started saying it to me and my sisters when we were young, and he'll still say it today if the occasion is right. When we would get frustrated or disheartened with a situation we were facing, he would say, "Remember, you're a Belihar…and Belihars never quit!" With those words, he impressed upon our hearts the value of never giving up and the importance of staying the course when dropping out would be much easier.

My dad taught me and my sisters what the apostle Paul knew, and what you and I must never forget: the only way to lose the race is to quit.

Finish Strong

The race is going to end for each of us. The Bible tells us that we will all face death and then after that, the judgment (Heb. 9:27). But Jesus eliminated all fear from that reality when he said, "He who endures until the end will be saved" (Matt. 10:22, 24:13). Whenever and wherever your finish might be, in order to finish strong, keep your eyes on Jesus. From beginning to end, throughout the entire race, always stay focused on Christ.

After encouraging his readers to run the race with endurance, the writer of Hebrews said this in Hebrews 12:2, "*Looking unto Jesus*, the author and finisher of our faith, who for the joy that was set before Him endured the cross, despising the shame, and has sat down at the right hand of the throne of God" (emphasis added). In this context, "looking" is used in the present tense participle form, indicating a continual action. The Greek word *aphorao* literally means "looking away from all else" or "to fix one's gaze upon." Looking to Jesus involves looking away from ourselves and from the distractions of the world. It's trusting him, listening to him, living for him, and following in his footsteps—which lead directly to the finish line.

Jesus is coming soon. Choose to run the race. Stay the course. Run to win. Finish strong.

"Behold, I am coming quickly! Hold fast what you have, that no one may take your crown" (Rev. 3:11).

THROUGH THE SPYGLASS

When the world sees the church, do they see people of endurance? Do they see people who never give up on their faith, even in the most difficult of circumstances? Does the world see a tribe of runners scaling mountains, navigating through swamps, trudging through deserts and praising God through it all? The world should see people who never give up on their faith, especially in times of trial. Christians should expect to experience pain and suffering in this life, and our response to those trials can send a message of faith and love to the watching world.

The world should see Christians enduring. This endurance is not just "getting through" the trial; it also involves the way we react to the trial. It's our ability to bear the situation but then adding to that our joyful hope. Endurance expresses glory in tribulation. It's how we can look past the pain we are experiencing and see, just beyond it, our eternal goal. Enduring is not something we can do without God. We have to trust in him and entrust everything we have to him. He will give us the strength and help we need to endure. When the world looks at the church, they should see people who never quit. They should see people who walk with God through the brightest days and the darkest days; glorifying him in both.

REFLECTIONS

- Why did God give man freewill?

- What did Paul mean when he said that the flesh wars against the spirit and the spirit against the flesh? How do we strengthen our spirits for this war?

- How do we enter the Christian "race?"

- What weights or sins do you need to lay aside so that you can run the race set before you?

- How do we keep our eyes focused on Jesus?

- Does that fact that "life is a vapor" affect how we run? In what way?

- There are going to be times when we might be tempted to give up on our faith. What can we do to keep from quitting? How do we find the ability to continue running?

- When the man on the island reached a breaking point, his fellow survivors were immediately there, surrounding him with comfort, encouragement, prayer, and hope. How are you helping other runners along the way? How have other runners helped you?

- What can we do to discipline ourselves as spiritual runners in the Christian race? (Read Paul's words in 1 Corinthians 9:24-27).

- In the Hope Preserver verse below, Paul wrote that we eagerly wait with perseverance for the hope we do not see. What is the relationship between hope and perseverance?

HOPE PRESERVER

"For we were saved in this hope, but hope that is seen is not hope; for why does one still hope for what he sees? But if we hope for what we do not see, we eagerly wait for it with perseverance" (Rom. 8:24-25).

MESSAGE IN A BOTTLE

The main idea of this chapter is that people of hope don't quit. They keep pressing on toward their goal. How does hope create this type of attitude? Describe how hope helps Christians persevere.

Dear friend,

CHAPTER 11

A HALF-FULL COCONUT!

Find joy

THE JOURNAL

Day Eleven: There is always joy.

I have found that despite the trials we have faced on this island, we have never lost our joy. Some may wonder how that is possible, and I will share two secrets my friends and I have learned in the short time we have been here: you must remember and you must rejoice.

Remember what is most important. Meditate on it and speak about it often. Keep it at the forefront of your mind so that it does not become buried beneath the mundane and the trivial. And, rejoice. Find small and large ways to show your joy. We may be stranded here, but we still have cause to celebrate. We are alive! What is it that we live for? We remember that, and we rejoice.

We have found our own ways to hold on to joy. It motivates us and it sustains us. We understand that time is short and the trials of this place will pass.

—Paul

"And not only that, but we also rejoice in God through our Lord Jesus Christ, through whom we have now received the reconciliation" (Rom. 5:11).

"Rejoice in the Lord always. Again I will say, rejoice!" (Phil. 4:4).

"Rejoice always" (1 Thess. 5:16).

THE SURVIVORS

Life on the island continued and each day was much the same as the one before. The survivors stayed busy because they had learned that sitting still for too long made the getting back to work much more difficult. Moving around, finding activities to do, and keeping their minds occupied also helped to keep sadness from creeping in and taking up residence in their hearts. Sometimes, even knowing that they would be going home one day was not enough to overcome the reality of their current circumstance, but they had discovered the same truth that Paul had described in the journal: remember and rejoice. They had to be intentional in holding on to their joy. So, to keep it alive within their group, they became a community of celebration. They rejoiced in everything!

Not only did this lift everyone's spirits, but it also provided more opportunities to use the gifts and talents represented in their group. They performed talent shows, had cooking contests, made sand sculptures, and invented new games. One game became their favorite—they called it "The Blessing Game." Everyone took turns naming a blessing, but each time they played the topic was different. It might be "The blessings of this island" or "The blessings of home" or "The blessings of this group." Sharing reminders of all the things that they could be thankful for had a wonderful way of renewing their joy.

Rejoicing also came in the smallest of moments: a shooting star, a perfectly ripe mango, a cool breeze from the ocean, a crackling fire, a great catch of fish. It was those little things that seemed to pull their joy right up to the surface of their hearts. But, the best rejoicing came every day when the survivors spent time in song and in prayer. It was in those times that their joy felt the most real, because they could actually see it in each other's faces and hear it as they lifted up their voices together.

THE CHURCH

Joy. The Merriam-Webster dictionary defines it as "the emotion evoked by well-being, success, or good fortune or by the prospect of possessing what one desires." This type of joy is what the world offers, and it's just a shadow of the true, enduring joy that we read about in the Bible. Biblical joy is an orientation of the heart, and it cannot be experienced apart from

God. It comes from standing firm and sure on the knowledge that God is our strength, our comfort, and our help no matter what circumstances we might face. The Christian's joy doesn't come and go depending on what is happening in a given moment. It stays. It doesn't leave, because God doesn't leave, and hope doesn't leave. Real joy takes residence in our hearts when we are settled in our faith and in our hope.

The joy of the Christian comes from God. "Now may the God of hope fill you with all joy and peace in believing, that you may abound in hope by the power of the Holy Spirit" (Rom. 15:13).

The joy of the Christian is found in Christ. "Rejoice in the Lord always. Again I will say, rejoice!" (Phil. 4:4).

The joy of the Christian is a fruit of the Spirit. "But the fruit of the Spirit is love, joy, peace, longsuffering, kindness, goodness, faithfulness, 23 gentleness, self-control. Against such there is no law" (Gal. 5:22-23).

God sent us his son Jesus: This is how he has given us irreplaceable joy.

Jesus reconciles us to our Father in heaven: This is how eternal joy is found in Christ.

The Holy Spirit works in our lives through the Word: This is how immeasurable joy is grown and produced by the Spirit.

Joy found in the world ultimately will not satisfy. Jesus knows that, and he wants so much for us to have the great joy that comes from being in him. And he doesn't just want us to have it in the smallest sense, or in a fleeting type of way. He wants our joy to be full (John 16:24), he wants it to remain in us (John 15:11), and he doesn't want it to be taken away by anyone (John 16:22).

"Rejoice in the Lord, you righteous, and give thanks at the remembrance of His holy name" (Psa. 97:12). As Christians, we are commanded to rejoice. That doesn't mean that we always feel happy, but we can rejoice even in sorrow and grief because joy doesn't depend on the emotions we are experiencing at a given point in time. Joy is the enduring, reassuring, unwavering truth that we are in Christ and have hope for a home in heaven for eternity.

Rejoice! We Are Children of God!

We have joy because by means of Jesus Christ we are now the adopted children of God! The apostle Paul wrote to the Ephesians, "Blessed be the God and Father of our Lord Jesus Christ, who has blessed us with every spiritual blessing in the heavenly places in Christ, just as He chose us in Him before the foundation of the world, that we should be holy and without blame before Him in love, having predestined us to adoption as sons by Jesus Christ to Himself, according to the good pleasure of His will" (Eph. 1:3-5). He chose his family before he ever created the world! He is the Father of the redeemed! Anyone can be his child through the blood of Jesus and have access to those marvelous blessings Paul goes on to describe in verses 7–14.

We have joy because we have been reborn through baptism! We were immersed in the water and died to our old selves, and then came up out of the water to walk in a new life! Through the waters of baptism, we contacted the blood of Jesus and we entered into a unique relationship with him. Baptism placed us "in" Christ—a place that we had to be in order to be adopted as children of God. But that's not all! In Christ we have forgiveness and redemption of sins. In Christ we have no condemnation. In Christ we have all spiritual blessings. In Christ we have an inheritance. In Christ we have salvation.

Because of Jesus, we are able to be members of God's household. We can't even comprehend the love of God in that he would give us that right (1 John 3:1; John 1:12). Whatever we've done in our past, like Paul, we can forget it and look ahead (Phil. 3:13-14), because if we have been baptized into Christ then we are now sons and daughters of God. We are a part of his family.

"Now, therefore, you are no longer strangers and foreigners, but fellow citizens with the saints and members of the household of God, having been built on the foundation of the apostles and prophets, Jesus Christ Himself being the chief cornerstone, in whom the whole building, being fitted together, grows into a holy temple in the Lord, in whom you also are being built together for a dwelling place of God in the Spirit" (Eph. 2:19-22).

This is reason to rejoice!

Rejoice! We Are Co-Heirs With Christ!

While at the tennis courts one day waiting for my daughters to finish up a lesson, I sat in the shade reading a book and my son played nearby with another little boy. They were close enough that I could hear their conversation and at one point the little boy asked Briggs, "Do you have a sister?" Briggs answered, "Actually, I have two sisters." His friend made a groaning sound and said, "Ugh. I feel sorry for you!" I wondered how Briggs would respond to that, although I know he thinks the world of his sisters. I could have cried when I heard him say, "Don't feel sorry for me! I feel lucky!"

Briggs finds joy in his relationship with Evie and Kate. He loves them dearly. I'm sure that when his little friend said that he felt sorry for him, Briggs thought back to the time his sisters decided to create their own "Brother's Day." I'm sure he thought about how they play with him and cheer him on at countless sporting events. He must have thought about the secret handshakes he shares with his sisters and how they encourage him in everything he does. He wasn't about to let someone think they should feel sorry for him for having sisters when he feels lucky! Since then, Briggs has learned that the good gifts in his life are much more than luck—they are blessings from God. When the world ridicules us for our faith, or looks down on us for being Christians, we should joyfully respond by saying, "We feel blessed!"

We have joy because of our relationship in Christ; we are now heirs of God! Paul mentioned this amazing promise in several of his letters. To the Christians in Rome, he wrote, "The Spirit Himself bears witness with our spirit that we are children of God, and if children, then heirs—heirs of God and joint heirs with Christ, if indeed we suffer with Him, that we may also be glorified together" (Rom. 8:16-17).

To the church in Galatia he wrote, "But when the fullness of the time had come, God sent forth His Son, born of a woman, born under the law, to redeem those who were under the law, that we might receive the adoption as sons. And because you are sons, God has sent forth the Spirit of His Son into your hearts, crying out, 'Abba, Father!' Therefore you are no longer a slave but a son, and if a son, then an heir of God through Christ" (Gal. 4:4-7). "And if you are Christ's, then you are Abraham's seed, and heirs according to the promise" (Gal. 3:29).

To the church in Colossae he wrote, "Giving thanks to the Father who has qualified us to be partakers of the inheritance of the saints in the light" (Col. 1:12). "And whatever you do, do it heartily, as to the Lord and not to men, knowing that from the Lord you will receive the reward of the inheritance; for you serve the Lord Christ" (Col. 3:24).

- We have joy because we have a future (Matt. 6:25-34).

- We have joy because we have a great reward (Matt. 5:12).

- We have joy because our names are written in heaven (Luke 10:20).

- We have joy because we have an inheritance and a reservation that is waiting for us there (1 Pet. 1:3-5).

These are all because of Jesus Christ and they are all reasons to rejoice!

Rejoice! We Are Wielders of the Spirit's Sword!

We have joy because we have in our hands the Spirit's sword, the wonderful Word of God! (Eph. 6:17; 2 Pet. 1:20-21). We should never underestimate this extraordinary gift we have been given! It's our source of truth (John 17:17). It reveals God's plan to save us. It contains everything we need to fully equip us for every good work (2 Tim. 3:16-17). It's an instruction manual for living in this world and a road map to show us the way to heaven. It's the means by which we establish and grow our faith (Rom. 10:17). It is as alive today as it was when it was breathed into being thousands of years ago, and it will endure forever! It continues day in and day out, powerfully working in the lives of people as it has for generations.

The Word of God is effectual; in other words, it will produce the desired results if it's applied correctly. It's sharp and piercing, even more than a sword, because with a single stroke it penetrates to the very center of who we are—laying open soul, spirit, joints, and marrow—to the deepest corners of our innermost beings. And there, it critically examines our thoughts and intentions and is fit to judge what it discovers (Heb. 4:12). While this is true, we must remember that the hands wielding this sword of the Spirit should do so carefully, lovingly, and humbly. The beautiful living Word, when planted in hearts, has the power to save souls (James 1:21). This places great responsibility on us as disciples of Jesus Christ!

Let's not leave our living, eternal, life-changing Bible unopened and unread. It's too powerful! It contains too much good and promises too much hope to not be lived and not be shared! We should take it with us every day as we go into battle, and whether we are defending or contending for our faith, we should always be sure to use it gently and respectfully (1 Pet. 3:15). The spiritual war we are enlisted in is difficult and dangerous, but we can have joy because we have an indestructible weapon, divinely-issued armor, and strength that comes from God (Eph. 6:10-17)!

The Word of God brings light, prosperity, and hope (Psa. 1:1-3, 119:105; Rom. 15:4). This is reason to rejoice!

Rejoice! We Have Access to the Throne of Grace!

We have joy because we can come before our Almighty God in prayer. The Hebrews writer said, "Let us therefore come boldly to the throne of grace, that we may obtain mercy and find grace to help in time of need" (Heb. 4:16). This is an invitation that we cannot take for granted. It's a privilege that is ours only because of Jesus and his sacrifice on the cross.

Under the Old Law, only the High Priest could enter the Holy of Holies into the presence of God. This honor was only reserved for one day out of the year—the Day of Atonement—in order to offer sacrifices for the sins of the people. No one else could step into that special place, and if the High Priest approached at any other time than what had been authorized—he would die. There must have been some degree of fear and apprehension that was experienced as the curtain was pulled back and the High Priest drew near to holiness. Then Jesus came and everything changed.

Through his death, Jesus, our Great High Priest, offered one sacrifice for sins forever and by his blood he provided eternal redemption. At his death, the inner veil of the temple was torn in two indicating that all can have access to God's holy presence, and not with fear and apprehension, but with boldness (Eph. 2:18)! This boldness, or confidence, is not in ourselves, but in Jesus, whose blood gives us the ability to come before

God and "pour our hearts out before him" (Heb. 10:20; Psa. 62:8). It's the blessing of standing before the throne of grace and speaking freely, without fear, about our needs, concerns, questions, and desires.

Not only can we approach God's throne confidently, but we can also know that Jesus is there always making intercession for us (Heb. 7:25). That means that he's continually pleading on our behalf because he understands our weaknesses and temptations (Heb. 4:15). And we can find comfort in knowing that God gives us help in our times of need with mercy (compassion and pardon) and grace (kindness and favor). This is reason to rejoice!

Rejoice! We Are Free From the Bondage of Sin!

We have joy because we are no longer slaves to sin! We've been set free! The chains have fallen and we are out of bondage! In baptism, we died to our sins and rose up out of the watery grave with a new life in Christ (Rom. 6:7). "But now having been set free from sin, and having become slaves of God, you have your fruit to holiness, and the end, everlasting life" (Rom. 6:22). We aren't slaves to uncleanness or lawlessness anymore! Now we are slaves to God, obedient to him and living according to his will.

Everyone is a slave to someone or something. This is what Paul said in Romans 6:16. We are either slaves to sin or slaves to obedience; one results in death and one results in righteousness. We choose which one we will serve. There's good news for the Christian found in Paul's words: "But God be thanked that though you were slaves of sin, yet you obeyed from the heart that form of doctrine to which you were delivered. And having been set free from sin, you became slaves of righteousness" (Rom. 6:17-18). Wholehearted obedience to the gospel leads to faith, repentance, confession of Jesus as the Son of God, and baptism into Jesus' death for the remission of sins. In the waters of baptism, we are washed with the blood of Jesus, and only his blood has the power to free us from the bonds of sin.

"Then Jesus said to those Jews who believed Him, 'If you abide in My word, you are My disciples indeed. And you shall know the truth, and the truth shall make you free.' They answered Him, 'We are Abraham's descendants, and have never been in bondage to anyone. How can You say, "You will be made free"?' Jesus answered them, 'Most assuredly, I say to you, whoever commits sin is a slave of sin. And a slave does not abide in the house forever, but a son abides forever. Therefore if the Son makes you free, you shall be free indeed'" (John 8:31-36).

We'll never live perfectly without sin, but we do have the promise that if we are faithful to the truth (abiding in his Word and walking in the light as he is in the light), and if we confess our sins, then he will forgive us and his blood will continually cleanse us. This is freedom! This is reason to rejoice!

THROUGH THE SPYGLASS

Does the world see joy when they look at the church? Do they see a joy that isn't fake, that doesn't depend on circumstances, or that isn't buried so deep that it's completely hidden? Do they see a people whose joy radiates from within and shines outward in their words and actions? With all of the pain, sadness, fear, and uncertainty in the world, the church must demonstrate something different, something infinitely better. We have to show the world the joy of who we are and who we are becoming. We are a saved people because of Jesus Christ, and we are becoming more and more like him every day as we strive to conform to his image. This is reason to rejoice!

Do we look like people who have been saved? Do we act like people who have been adopted by the Almighty Creator of the universe and have an inheritance waiting for us in heaven? We have a joy that the world cannot fully understand! We need to live so that they see us and say, "We want that kind of joy! A joy that never goes away!" The world should see Jesus when they see the church. We are imitators of him and he is a rejoicer! Jesus endured the cross "for the joy that was set before him!" (Heb. 12:2). He looked past the cross, and beyond it, he saw the joy of bringing salvation to mankind. That was his JOY! How much more should we share in that joy knowing that our Lord and Savior has already paid the price for our sins? We have every reason to be the most joyous people on the earth. Let the world see us rejoice!

REFLECTIONS

- What is the difference in happiness and joy? (Consider that the root word hap- means "chance").

- Think of the most joy-filled person you know. What makes him or her joyful? How do they live in a way that demonstrates their joy?

- What is joy for the Christian?

- What can steal our joy? Can it be lost or stolen?

- How does one become a child of God? What are some of the blessings that come from that relationship (Eph. 1:3-14)?

- Rejoicing was a daily and intentional practice among the survivors on the island. How do you rejoice as a Christian? Is it something you do outwardly?

- What challenges do we face daily that make it difficult to express our joy?

- How can we hold on to our joy in times of sadness or grief?

- In what way does the Word of God bring us joy?

- In the Hope Preserver verse below there is a connection made between hope, joy, and peace. How does hope affect our joy?

HOPE PRESERVER

"Now may the God of hope fill you with all joy and peace in believing, that you may abound in hope by the power of the Holy Spirit" (Rom. 15:13).

MESSAGE IN A BOTTLE

The main idea of this chapter is that people of hope are people of joy. Write a note to someone explaining why hope and joy go hand-in-hand. How would you describe their connection to someone?

FINDING SEASHELLS

The book of Psalms is overflowing with songs of rejoicing. Some examples are Psalms 8, 9, 29, 47, 66, 96, 98, 100, 111, 117, 135, and 145 – 150. Spend time reading those psalms, and then write your own joyful psalm to the Lord. Make it as short or as long as you like and on any topic that you choose. This is a great spiritual exercise to practice from time to time! Try writing psalms of gratitude, contentment, fear, love, sorrow, or any other emotion you might be experiencing. It can be truly faith-building.

Dear friend,

CHAPTER 12

THERE'S TREASURE HERE!

Discover extraordinary love

THE JOURNAL

Day Twelve: Amazing love.

Of all the notes I have made since my days on the island began, this one is perhaps of the greatest importance. Today, I am writing about love. Without it, I am not certain I would have the will to write. I believe with all of my heart that love is what has kept our hope for rescue alive! My desire is for my companions to be saved from this island. I desire it to such an extent that I would give my life to that end. But here is the truth of the matter—my friends desire the same for me and would give their lives for me as well. This is why we are not *only surviving, but we are living to the fullest.*

It is because of love that we have worked together, used each other's talents, helped each other, sought peace, persevered through challenges, held onto our joy, and have continued to remind each other about home. Love has bound us together here on the island, and I know that we will carry it with us whenever we leave this place. Never neglect love. Instead, pursue it!

—Paul

"Love suffers long and is kind; love does not envy; love does not parade itself, is not puffed up; does not behave rudely, does not seek its own, is not provoked, thinks no evil; does not rejoice in iniquity, but rejoices in the truth; bears all things, believes all things, hopes all things, endures all things" (1 Cor. 13:4-7).

"Pursue love…" (1 Cor. 14:1)

"But above all these things put on love, which is the bond of perfection" (Col. 3:14).

THE SURVIVORS

The captain stood at the edge of the ocean, looking out over the water. He reflected on all that had taken place since crawling onto the sand beneath his feet almost two weeks ago. It seemed surreal. Had they really been on this island for that long? He thought about the how the group had boarded a ship as strangers and how much had changed since then. Something had happened between the survivors—something unique, something strange and wonderful.

He turned around to face the beach. To his left he saw a group of women sitting in a circle, talking and laughing together. To his right he saw some men and boys playing football with a papaya. He saw several people talking together outside the huts, a few people preparing the fish for supper, and children digging in the sand. He saw an older man showing a younger man how to carve a spoon out of a piece of wood, and a family walking arm in arm along the shoreline. Many of these people had not known each other before the island and seeing their relationships now brought the captain to tears.

There was only one word that could define the change that had occurred on the island, and that word was love. The survivors had grown to love each other. Not just superficially or emotionally, but with the deep, unconditional agape love that seeks the highest good for someone else. The journal had revealed that Paul and his companions had experienced it, too.

Taking in the view of the beach again, the captain didn't simply see the people; this time he saw strength, peace, kindness, selflessness, courage, endurance, and rising above it all, he saw extraordinary love. Hope is what kept them surviving, but love is what kept them living.

THE CHURCH

Christianity is built on love. It's the very foundation of our faith. Love is the reason we have hope because love is the reason Jesus came to earth. "For God so loved the world that He gave His only begotten Son that whoever believes in Him should not perish but have everlasting life" (John 3:16). Love is the reason we have hope because love is the reason Jesus went to the cross. "But God demonstrates His own love toward us, in that while we were still sinners, Christ died for us." (Rom. 5:8). Without love, nothing else matters.

The apostle John wrote a great deal on the subject of love in his first epistle. He talked about God's love for us, our love for God, and the love that we have for others. It's been said that when John grew old and was working with the church in Ephesus, he would begin each period of worship with the saints by standing up and declaring, "Little children, love one another." That's a story that comes from secular history, not Scripture, but it's certainly in keeping with John's writings. He knew the importance of love as he himself had sat at the feet of Jesus and heard him say "A new commandment I give to you, that you love one another; as I have loved you that you also love one another. By this all will know that you are My disciples, if you have love for one another" (John 13:34-35).

Agape is the Greek word that is used to describe the love that is of God and from God. 1 John 4:8 tells us that God's very nature is love. Agape is also used to describe our love for God (Luke 10:27), the love we are to have for others (John 13:34), and even the love that we extend to our enemies (Matt. 5:44). Agape love is defined as sacrificial love. Jesus said, "Greater love has no one that this, than to lay down one's life for his friends" (John 15:13). A love that is willing to die for another, even if that person is unworthy, sinful, or an enemy, is the most supreme form of love. It's a God-type of love that doesn't naturally come from within you and me. It's only because of Christ in us that we can know that kind of love (Eph. 3:17-18). It's a love that urges us to seek the highest good for someone else—without expecting anything in return.

Love is the umbrella under which all other commandments stand. When

Jesus was questioned about the greatest commandment in the law, he answered, "'You shall love the Lord your God with all your heart, with all your soul, and with all your mind.' This is the first and great commandment. And the second is like it: 'You shall love your neighbor as yourself.' On these two commandments hang all the Law and the Prophets" (Matt. 22:37-40). It all comes back to love. If the church has hope, it's only because it first has love.

Love is Powerful

Love is powerful because it extends beyond the boundary of this world. In the final verse of 1 Corinthians 13, Paul wrote, "And now abide faith, hope, and love, these three; but the greatest of these is love" (1 Cor. 13:13). Love is greater than faith and hope because love is the foundation of all. Without love, our faith and hope are nothing. One day, our hope will be realized at the return of Jesus and our faith will be sight, but our love will continue, in a perfect sense, as our everlasting motivation for worshiping and praising our God in heaven.

- Love is powerful because it can overcome pain, discouragement, and hopelessness.

- Love powerfully binds and knits people together.

- Love is the power behind our faith.

- Love has the power to endure all things and it never fails.

- Love is powerful because it builds people up.

God is love and there is nothing and no one more powerful than God. When we are filled with the fullness of God, as a result of Christ being settled in our hearts and as a result of the strengthening of our inner man through God's Word, we will begin to see the power of his love in our lives, and it will be more than we could ever ask or imagine (Eph. 3:16-20).

In its strongest expression—one that changed the course of history and affected our eternal destination—love conquered death! "Thanks be to God, who gives us the victory through our Lord Jesus Christ" (1 Cor. 15:57).

Love is Selfless

Love is selfless because it sacrifices. Love always looks to the best interest of others. Love wants everyone to have the hope of heaven. Love empties itself, just as Jesus did when he came to this world. Philippians 2:7-8, says that "He made himself of no reputation, taking the form of a bondservant, and coming in the likeness of men. And being found in appearance as a man, He humbled Himself and became obedient to the point of death, even the death of the cross." Love strives to have the same attitude as Jesus.

- Love is gracious and merciful.

- Love doesn't criticize or keep a record of past mistakes.

- Love looks for ways to build people up.

- Love doesn't keep score and doesn't insist on having its way.

- Love listens.

Learning, living, and spreading selfless love is a priority for Christians. It's how we show the world who Jesus is and what it means to be a child of God. Listen to Paul's words to the believers in Philippi: "Let nothing be done through selfish ambition or conceit, but in lowliness of mind let each esteem others better than himself. Let each of you look out not only for his own interests, but also for the interests of others" (Phil. 2:3-4). Love is about pouring yourself out so that you can fill others up.

Love is Boundless

Love is boundless in that it extends from family, to friends, to neighbors, and even to enemies. Understanding that we are all made in the image of God, love sees the value of every human being. Love is not offered to some and withheld from others; it is given freely. Love sees past the outward appearance and looks at the heart, seeing all people as God sees all people—worthy of kindness and compassion and having been created in his image.

- Love cannot be measured, it cannot be contained, and it cannot be bound by time or place.

- Love has no borders.

- Love forgives again and again.

- Love hopes and anticipates the best.

- Love is eternal.

Boundless love can be most clearly seen in the cross of Calvary. With arms extended open, reaching from eternity to eternity drawing all of mankind to him, Jesus was crucified because of a love so deep, so high, so wide, and so long that it surpasses knowledge (Eph. 3:18-19). His immeasurable love pulled us out of the pit of sin and raised us up into the heavenly places where we have been blessed with every spiritual blessing (Eph. 1:3). Jesus teaches us that love is not limited by anything.

Love is Active

Love doesn't only say things, love does them. In his first letter, the apostle

John wrote, "My little children, let us not love in word or in tongue, but in deed and in truth" (1 John 3:18). Love is an action. It's a choice we make to put the needs of others above our own. It's given with a spirit of willing sacrifice, in the name of Jesus. Love is also true. That means that our actions aren't just for show. Love comes from a sincere and obedient heart, and is extended to others with kindness and joy.

- Love walks hand-in-hand with good works.

- Love compels us to obey God.

- Love sees a need and fills it.

- Love perseveres and doesn't give up on people.

- Love is faithful.

Love is work. The Hebrews writer said, "For God is not unjust to forget your work and labor of love which you have shown toward His name, in that you have ministered to the saints, and do minister" (Heb. 6:10). As Christians, our "labor of love" is serving each other, bearing each other's burdens, forgiving each other, praying for each other, edifying each other, encouraging each other, providing for each other, confessing our sins to each other, rejoicing with each other, teaching each other, leading each other, and showing mercy and grace to each other. Jesus said that the world will know that we are his disciples if we have love for one another (John 13:35). There's truth behind the words we sing: "They'll know we are Christians by our love." Love sets us apart as followers of Jesus, but the world has to see it in our actions!

Love is Peculiar

Agape love is peculiar because it's so different from the world's perception of love. The world says, "I'll love you if you do something for me," and

"I love you, but not enough to give up what I want." The world's love is conditional. Fickle. Wrapped up in selfishness and pride. It's completely counter to the love of God and the love we are to have as Christians. The world's love makes no changes, takes no chances, and accepts no responsibilities. It's easy! Agape love, on the other hand, takes us to difficult places, pushes us out of our comfortable chairs, and asks us to give up everything. It's not easy, but it promises the greatest reward.

- Love sees the best in people.

- Love is not critical.

- Love doesn't take revenge.

- Love forgives the unforgivable.

- Love seeks peace.

The world should see Christians practicing a unique love. Jesus' love involved foot washing, eating with sinners, touching the diseased, befriending the poor, and accepting the rejected. His love was distinctive. It was unlike anything the world had seen before. The gospel calls us to have the same kind of love. God designates us as his "peculiar people" (1 Pet. 2:9 KJV), and as such, we should practice a peculiar love.

THROUGH THE SPYGLASS

Looking at the church, the world should see love. They should see a powerful, selfless, boundless, active, and peculiar love. They should see a love that makes them think of Jesus! This is not just important— it's necessary. If we want to share the message of the gospel with the world, they have to see that our motivation is love. They have to see that the love extended from the church is different than the love that is found in the world. They have to see a completely selfless love. The love of Christians is a love that says, "I want the very best for you!" It's a love that says, "You are valuable to God and you are valuable to me." It's a love that says, "Do you know Jesus? He will change your life. Can I share with you what he has done for me?"

When the world sees the church, they should see love in action! We must be a people who back up our words of love with good works. The world should see our love, but they should also experience it. They should be recipients of our kindness and witnesses of our patience. They should also see love within the church being demonstrated among Christians. Jesus said that this is how the world would know that we are his disciples—by our love for each other (John 13:34-35).

Each member of the church that belongs to Jesus Christ is responsible for spreading his love in the world. If we really want to know what the world sees when it looks at the church, we should begin by looking at ourselves. Does the world see love when it looks at you and me?

REFLECTIONS

- How do we define the type of love that God has shown for us and the love that he expects for us to have for others? In what way(s) is this love fundamental to Christianity?

- Can we love apart from the truth? Why or why not?

- How does the church promote love in the world? Are Christians known as people who extend love? Why did love grow to such a great measure among the survivors on the island?

- Does love have a limit? How long do we remain patient with someone who is living in sin or who continues to violate our trust?

- How can we come to be known as people who persevere in love? How can the church be known in that way?

- What is our motivation for working in the kingdom?

- What do the first three verses of 1 Corinthians 13 tell us about the importance of love?

- In what specific ways do we demonstrate love for our brothers and sisters in Christ? How about our neighbors? Our enemies?

- Why is love greater than faith and hope (1 Cor. 13:13)?

- In reference to the Hope Preserver verse below, what relationship does our hope have with the love of God being poured out in our hearts?

HOPE PRESERVER

"Now hope does not disappoint, because the love of God has been poured out in our hearts by the Holy Spirit who was given to us" (Rom. 5:5).

MESSAGE IN A BOTTLE

The main idea of this chapter is that hope filled people discover extraordinary love. How can you explain the hope and love that fill the life of someone who is in Christ? Christians hope because of love and love because of hope. Describe how one complements and strengthens the other.

Dear friend,

CHAPTER 13

DON'T GET ATTACHED TO THE ISLAND!

Remember your home

THE JOURNAL

Day Thirteen: Home.

On this day, I write my farewell. We have been rescued! A ship has come and we are going home. Home. To me there is not a more beautiful word. Thinking back on all that has happened here, all that we have suffered, all that we have endured, I realize in this moment that it was nothing—it was fleeting. And now I am going home. I cannot imagine the reunion that awaits! I know that it will be grand. I know that it will be joyful. I know that it will be marked with love, and tears, and embracing. How I have longed for home!

I may never know if this journal is found. I leave it here with the hope that something that I have written will help another. If this journal is right now in the hands of a survivor, I charge you with this: Do not live for the island... live for whatever it is that you hope for.

Peace be with you.

—Paul

"But now having been set free from sin, and having become slaves of God, you have your fruit to holiness, and the end, everlasting life. For the wages of sin is death, but the gift of God is eternal life in Christ Jesus our Lord" (Rom. 6:22-23).

"For I consider that the sufferings of this present time are not worthy to be compared with the glory which shall be revealed to us" (Rom. 8:18).

"For our citizenship is in Heaven from which we also eagerly wait for the Savior, the Lord Jesus Christ, who will transform our lowly body that it may be conformed to His glorious body, according to the working by which He is able even to subdue all things to Himself" (Phil. 3:20).

THE SURVIVORS

There was no denying the beauty of the island. With white sand next to turquoise water, palm trees and brightly colored flowers, mountains for a back drop and clear blue skies overhead, it was like a picture from a travel book. The sunrises and sunsets were breathtaking. The fruit was sweet. There were no pressures and no deadlines.

On the evening of the thirteenth day, the group had just eaten a meal together and enjoyed a time of games and singing. A fire had been built, there was a cool breeze coming off of the water, and way in the distance a school of porpoises jumped the ocean waves. Island birds were just beginning their chorus of night songs and the first stars were appearing in the twilight sky.

"Now I could get used to this," one man announced as he put his hands behind his head and leaned back onto the sand. "I think I might be happy to stay right here for good."

Another survivor who was standing close by heard those words and sat down next to his friend in the sand. He didn't say anything for a few minutes. He thought about the island and some of the blessings they had encountered here. He looked at his friend who had his eyes closed and seemed to be soaking up the pleasure of the moment. He reached over and put his hand on his friend's shoulder. "You're right. It's a beautiful place," he said. "But, remember the words from the journal: We're not from here. We're going home, and home is far, far better. We know rescue is coming, maybe weeks from now, maybe tomorrow. We don't know. So, enjoy moments like this one, my friend. Just don't forget your home."

THE CHURCH

Heaven. Our home and our hope. We may be in this world now, but we're on our way to something better! Here, we are pilgrims, just passing through. We have on our traveling shoes, with the Bible as our road map, and our sights set on the Promised Land. Christians look at this life through eternal lenses and they know that the best is yet to come!

Heaven. We can know that we're going! This knowledge is not based on emotions, or guessing, or man's opinions, but on the right relationship with the Son of God. Romans 6:23 says, "For the wages of sin is death, but the gift of God is eternal life in Christ Jesus our Lord." The apostle John makes the same statement in 1 John 5:11-12, "And this is the testimony that God has given us eternal life, and this life is in His Son. He who has the Son has life; he who does not have the Son of God does not have life." The question then becomes, "Are you in Christ?" If the answer is "yes" and you live faithfully according to God's Word, then the precious gift of eternal life belongs to you!

God has told us clearly in his Word how to get "into" Christ. Paul wrote these words to Christians in Rome, "Or do you not know that as many of us as were baptized into Christ Jesus were baptized into His death?" (Rom. 6:3). Using similar words to the church in Galatia he wrote, "For as many of you as have been baptized into Christ have put on Christ" (Gal. 3:27). In Christ, we are in his body (Eph. 2:16), which is his church (Eph. 1:22-23), of which he is the Savior (Eph. 5:23). In Christ, there is redemption and forgiveness of sins (Eph. 1:7), there are spiritual blessings (Eph. 1:3), there is eternal salvation (Acts 4:12), and there is no condemnation (Rom. 8:1). Our hope is found in Jesus Christ! We can confidently expect to be saved because we are in Christ, and he is in us, and he is taking us to heaven for eternity.

Heaven. How can we even begin to understand its magnificence? We can't adequately describe it because of our inability to comprehend it! There are not words in our language or images in our mind that can do justice to the glory and majesty of heaven. But there is enough revealed in Scripture to make us want to go there. Not just want to go there, but long to go there! Our hope is laid up for us in heaven (Col. 1:5). We don't doubt our future, and we aren't uncertain about tomorrow. We confidently expect and happily anticipate the beautiful place called heaven.

It's Prepared For Us

As his appointment with death was nearing, Jesus spent time with his disciples, covering them with words of encouragement and comfort. In John 14:1-4, he said to them, "Let not your heart be troubled; you believe in God, believe also in Me. In My Father's house are many mansions; if it were not so, I would have told you. I go to prepare a place for you. And if I go and prepare a place for you, I will come again and receive you to Myself; that where I am, there you may be also. And where I go you know, and the way you know." Two times in these verses, Jesus referred to a place that he was going, and he assured his disciples that one day they would be with him again in that place.

That place is heaven! It's where God is (Matt. 6:9), and it's where Jesus ascended when he left this earth (Acts 1:11). David wrote in Psalm 11:4, "The Lord is in His holy temple, the Lord's throne is in Heaven; His eyes behold. His eyelids test the sons of men." God is on his throne in heaven and Jesus is sitting at his right hand (Heb. 12:2), and they want you and me to be there with them in that place! The wonderful truth is that if you are in Christ, then you already have a reservation (1 Pet. 1:4)! Your name is already written in the book of life (Rev. 20:15)!

If you are not yet in Christ, he is inviting you to come (Rev. 3:20). Jesus is knocking at the door waiting for you to open it and let him in! It's been said, "Heaven is a prepared place for a prepared people." Jesus has done his part; be sure that you have made the right preparations, too!

It's a Better Country

In his letter to the church in Philippi, speaking about his life and his death, Paul wrote, "For I am hard-pressed between the two, having a desire to depart and be with Christ, which is far better" (Phil. 1:23). Paul looked forward to the day he would be with Christ. He hoped for it! He knew that it would be far better than anything in this life. In that same letter after telling his fellow Christians to follow his example, Paul said, "For our citizenship is in heaven, from which we also eagerly wait for the Savior, the Lord Jesus Christ, who will transform our lowly body that it may be conformed to His glorious body, according to the working by which He is able even to subdue all things to Himself" (Phil. 3:20-21).

Like Abraham, we are strangers and pilgrims on this earth who desire a better, heavenly country (Heb. 11:13-16). The good news for Christians is that because of Jesus Christ, our citizenship is already there! God has promised heaven, and God always keeps his promises. In Hebrews 11:10, we read that Abraham was waiting for a city built by God and a few verses later we read that God has prepared that city. It's a city that God's faithful people are still seeking (Heb. 13:14).

One day we'll be there in that holy city! It's beautifully described in the last two chapters of the book of Revelation. "There shall be no night there: They need no lamp nor light of the sun, for the Lord God gives them light and they shall reign forever and ever" (Rev. 22:5). By far the greatest joy that we can anticipate in that glorious city and heavenly country is that we will live with God there. "He will dwell with them, and they shall be His people" (Rev. 21:3). How can we even begin to imagine a place so wonderful?

It's Your Inheritance

In heaven, we have an inheritance that is waiting for us. If we are in Christ, then we are the adopted children of God and therefore co-heirs with Jesus Christ. According to Colossians 1:12, God has qualified us to be partakers of this inheritance by means of his Son, and he has promised that we will receive that reward (Col. 3:23-25; Heb. 9:15). In his first epistle, Peter explained to Christians that because of Jesus, we have been born again to a living hope and to an inheritance "incorruptible and undefiled and that does not fade away, reserved in heaven for you, who are kept by the power of God through faith for salvation ready to be revealed in the last time" (1 Pet. 1:3-5).

Our inheritance is incorruptible. This means that it's not subject to decay or destruction. We enjoy physical blessings in this life, but they don't last forever. They can be lost or stolen. They can rust or break. Eventually, they will be completely gone because they are only temporary. Even our own bodies are in the process of dying. But, our inheritance in heaven is everlasting! It will never go away!

Our inheritance is undefiled. This means that it's pure. Even the most beautiful and amazing things found in this world have some degree of imperfection. That's just the nature of the world we live in. Only Christ lived perfectly while he was here, and the reward that we have in him is characterized in the same way: holy and blameless. Our inheritance in heaven is completely perfect! It will never spoil or stain!

Our inheritance is unfading. This means that it will endure forever. It won't just endure in the sense that it won't die, but also in the sense that it will never lose its original brightness and beauty. Our world is filled with all different types of flowers. Although they are lovely to look at, their colors will fade and they will eventually wither. This is not the case with our heavenly inheritance! It will never depreciate. It will shine as intensely as it does today for all of eternity!

Because we hope for our incorruptible, undefiled, and unfading inheritance, we can speak the words of David found in Psalm 16:5-6, "O Lord, you are the portion of my inheritance and my cup; You maintain my lot. The lines have fallen to me in pleasant places; yes, I have a good inheritance."

It's All Good

We may not fully understand what heaven will look like or feel like until we experience it spiritually, but we can know without a doubt, that everything about heaven is going to be good. There will be nothing dark or evil there. When we leave this world, we will leave behind suffering, hate, temptation, guilt, futility—all of those things that came into the world with the first sin. We will be with God, who is the very essence of love, joy, peace, patience, kindness, goodness, faithfulness, gentleness, and self-control. This is why Paul believed that death would be gain (Phil. 1:21). He knew that on the other side of this life he would be with Christ and everything would be good.

It's a place of rest. "Come to Me, all you who labor and are heavy laden, and I will give you rest. Take My yoke upon you and learn from Me, for I am gentle and lowly in heart, and you will find rest for your souls" (Matt. 11:28-29). Heaven provides a blessed, everlasting rest. "Then I heard a voice from heaven saying to me, 'Write: Blessed are the dead who die in the Lord from now on.' 'Yes,' says the Spirit, 'that they may rest from their labors, and their works follow them'" (Rev. 14:13).

It's a place of reward. "Rejoice and be exceedingly glad, for great is your reward in Heaven, for so they persecuted the prophets who were before you" (Matt. 5:12). It's the place where we'll hear the words "Well done, good and faithful servant…Enter into the joy of your lord" (Matt. 25:23).

It's a place of no sin, no pain, no death, no sorrows, and no tears. "And God will wipe away every tear from their eyes; there shall be no more death, nor sorrow, nor crying. There shall be no more pain, for the former things have passed away" (Rev. 21:4). The struggles of this life and the evils of this world will no longer cause us pain. "Its gates will not be shut at all by day (there shall be no night there). And they shall bring the glory and the honor of the nations into it. But there shall by no means enter it anything that defiles, or causes an abomination or a lie, but only those who are written in the Lamb's Book of Life" (Rev. 21:25-27).

Imagine a place so wonderful! Imagine reuniting with all of the people we love so much who have gone before us. Imagine worshiping and praising in the very presence of God and the sound of his voice singing over us. Imagine having an incorruptible, immortal spiritual body in the very image of Christ. A place of such perfect goodness is more than the heart can even comprehend!

And It's Eternal

Life eternal is forever without end. It's a gift that is only found in Jesus Christ (Rom. 6:23), who is the source of our eternal salvation (Heb. 5:9). Near the end of his first letter, the apostle John wrote, "And this is the testimony: that God has given us eternal life, and this life is in His Son. He who has the Son has life: he who does not have the Son of God does not have life" (1 John 5:11-12). To have the hope of eternal life in heaven, we have to have the right relationship with Jesus Christ: we have to be in him. We also have to remain there. We have to "abide in him" and if we do, then we have the promise of eternal life (1 John 2:24-25).

Every soul has an eternal destination. At the end of the parable of the sheep and the goats, Jesus said, "And these will go away into everlasting punishment, but the righteous into eternal life" (Matt. 25:46). One destination is punishment and the other is life. Jesus said he came to give us an abundant life: a life that is continuous, on-going, exceeding the limit! (John 10:10). That life is found eternally in Christ. If you are in him, then that's where your hope resides. Hope in Christ is the confident expectation and a happy anticipation of his return, when he will take his church home.

Be strong and stay faithful, friend, rescue is coming.

THROUGH THE SPYGLASS

When the world looks at the church, do they see people who are traveling home? Do they see men and women who are laying up treasures in heaven? Do they see people who are fully assured that one day they will be there? They should! They should see confident Christians, who boldly proclaim, "We ARE going to see The King someday!" They should see Christians whose hope is so sure that they can't help but share the reason why. They should see Christians who know where they're going, not because of a hunch, or a feeling, but because of their relationship in Jesus Christ as a result of their true and genuine biblical faith.

The mission of the church is to share the gospel, with a desire to find the lost and tell them what they need to know in order to be saved. Our goal is eternal life in heaven, not only for us, but also for the rest of the world. It's the highest good we could want for anyone. To help people get there is the truest expression of love. We live in a world that desperately needs hope. There are lost souls who need to know that life on this earth is not the end. There's something better still to come. Maybe if we live like people who are confidently expecting to be with Jesus one day…maybe if we live like we are citizens of a better country…maybe if we live like we are heirs of an incorruptible inheritance…maybe if we live like we are happily anticipating an eternal life in a place that is only everything good…maybe if we live like a people of hope, the world will notice, and they will open up their hearts to the truth.

REFLECTIONS

- What does it mean to "lay up treasures in Heaven?" How do we do that?

- Remember this reminder spoken from one survivor to another: "We're not from here. We're going home, and home is far, far better."

What do you long for the most when you think about the promises of heaven?

- How does a confident expectation for heaven affect the way that Christians live their lives? How does it affect the work of the church?

- How can we be sure that we are going to heaven?

- What did Jesus mean in Luke 17:20-21, when he said "The kingdom of God does not come with observation; nor will they say, 'See here!' or 'See there!' For indeed, the kingdom of God is within you"?

- In "The Survivors" section of most chapters in this study, prayer was incorporated as a regular part of the survivors' lives on the island. What is the importance of prayer when it comes to our hope? What is the role of prayer in the lives of Christians? Why do we pray?

- What answer would you give someone who asks about the reason for your hope (1 Pet. 3:15)? What does it mean to give your answer with "meekness and fear"?

- In the Hope Preserver verse below, how does hope relate to the truth of the gospel? Is it possible to have biblical hope without knowing, understanding, and responding in faithful obedience to the gospel?

- Reflecting back on this entire study, consider the meaning behind the following: the name of the ship that went down in the storm (hint... "Sarx" is a Greek word), the number of days the survivors spent in the water, the number of survivors, fourteen total days spent on the island. How do these symbols enrich the theme of the study?

- How has this study impacted your understanding of biblical hope? In what way has it influenced your view on how the church represents hope in the world? What is something specific that you have gained from this study that has impacted you spiritually or that will help you in your daily walk?

HOPE PRESERVER

"...because of the hope which is laid up for you in heaven, of which you heard before in the word of the truth of the gospel" (Col. 1:5).

MESSAGE IN A BOTTLE

The main idea of this final chapter is that hope thinks about home. The hope of the Christian involves a confident expectation that heaven awaits. It is our happy anticipation that there is more to come after this life. Write a note to the world that describes your hope for eternal life. On what do you base your hope? And what do you look forward to the most about your home in heaven?

FINDING SEASHELLS

What do you do to keep your mind focused on your heavenly home? How do you continue to "set your mind on things above" (Col. 3:2)? Let me encourage you to make prayer and Bible study a part of your everyday routine. If we are going to be transformed by the renewing of our minds, it is essential that we immerse ourselves in the book given to us by God. I'm going to challenge you to begin a spirit-focused journal. In that journal you can write down prayer requests you've received from others or your own daily prayer focus. You can record what you studied in your personal Bible study time, or verses you want to meditate on, or spiritual goals you are striving to accomplish. It's a journal for your "inner self." Start one today.

Dear friend,

The sounding of a horn!

Was it real? Could they have just imagined it?

Again! It was real!

Survivors began stumbling out of the woods and onto the beach. Huts were left deserted, nets were dropped, and fruit fell from cradled arms. Legs crashed through shallow waves and hands shielded eyes as they looked out over the water into the sun.

The outline of a ship!

Some splashed in the ocean waters and others collapsed to their knees on the sand. Some yelled in joyful celebration while others held their tear-streaked faces and silently cried.

It was there: the moment for which they had all been waiting, surviving, and hoping.

The promise was fulfilled...

Rescue had come.

> *"For this we say to you by the word of the Lord, that we who are alive and remain until the coming of the Lord will by no means precede those who are asleep. For the Lord Himself will descend from heaven with a shout, with the voice of an archangel, and with the trumpet of God. And the dead in Christ will rise first. Then we who are alive and remain shall be caught up together with them in the clouds to meet the Lord in the air. And thus we shall always be with the Lord,*

therefore comfort one another with these words" (1 Thess. 4:15-18).

"Come quickly, Lord Jesus" (Rev. 22:20).

Made in the USA
Columbia, SC
29 August 2018